To Jessica
From Theressa Crain

Go Out With Joy

Go Out
With Joy

NORMA YOUNG STEVENS

BROADMAN PRESS · Nashville, Tennessee

DEWEY DECIMAL CLASSIFICATION NUMBER: 266.092
Library of Congress catalog card number: 66-19905
Printed in the United States of America
13.AT66KSP

Go Out With Joy

Chapter 1

The heat from the concrete runway blasted my face as I staggered under the weight of an oversize handbag. It was loaded to the brim with personal belongings jumbled together with odds and ends the children had poked in at the last minute. I held on with my free hand to the black taffeta hat perched precariously on my head and looked back at Howard.

He had his pockets so loaded he was wobbling from side to side trying to keep his briefcase and camera from bouncing against all the lumps. He managed to grin and jerked his head in the direction of Cathy and Karen. They were trailing the rear, dragging their plastic bags beside them. These were crammed with junk I had thrown out, hopefully, only to be informed that the discards were the most important things they owned . . . "didn't you know?" After that they repacked them, sitting on the floor behind the bed so I couldn't see what was going in.

We weren't trying to gyp the airline. All we were carrying had been left over after we packed. The official checking our luggage had looked at us with amusement. We were several pounds overweight already, so he tactfully ignored the obvious extras. And the stewardess said nothing either but clapped her hands to her forehead when she caught sight of the parade that thumped and bumped up the steps to the plane.

We inched our way into the seats she pointed out and tried to settle down. The large cabin was filled with people leaving New Orleans, as we were, for San José, Costa Rica, or one of the other Central American countries. Howard checked his pockets for the tickets and started to lean back. He looked again and then asked me, "Where did you put the passports, Norma?"

"Where did *I* put the passports? I haven't even had them!" The little squeak that punctuated my answer spoke volumes. It meant, "Stop kidding! Are you trying to scare me to death?"

Unfortunately he wasn't teasing. He stood and began a methodical search from pocket to pocket. His efforts were hampered by all the things he had loaded in each pocket. Then he took out his briefcase and began to look in it.

By this time many of the people around us had become interested. They looked under the seats and in the aisle, all the time murmuring things meant to help, such as, "You know you can't leave the plane when we arrive without your passports," and "Buddy, do you have any idea how much time it takes to get new ones? I lost mine once in Italy and, friend, let me tell you, I was stuck." And on it went. Howard didn't bother to answer. He turned to me and said, "Will you please look?" His asperity hit home, and I reluctantly opened up my purse.

It was almost as big as a train case, and I had tried to pack things in it in the order which I thought they might be needed. As I jumbled through everything, all my order dissolved into chaos, and I still didn't see the passports. "You see? Not here!"

Cathy had gotten out of her seat and was visiting someone down the aisle. When she came back and saw the confusion, she asked, "What are you looking for, Daddy?" At eight she had already begun to develop a sense of responsibility for her father. Karen, three, was totally uninvolved. She was busily coloring, an occupation that was intended to pass the time for her while in the air, but one that was dispatched before the plane left the ground. After takeoff she had no more interest in the book.

In answer to Cathy, Howard grunted, "The passports, Sugar," and went on looking. My pessimistic inner eye already had us off the plane and headed back to town. The thought of taking a later flight wasn't exactly to my liking. We were expected in Costa Rica the following day to register for classes at the Spanish Language School in San Jose. And as new missionaries of the Foreign Mission Board of the Southern Baptist Convention we were a little awed by the responsibility. This was the same feeling that we had had from the beginning, from the first moment when we felt a definite call to missionary service. There was elation, joy and wonderment, intermingled with a deep concern that we not fail Christ who loved us so. I thought fiercely: We just can't start off on such a wrong foot!

The motors of the plane began to turn over. The lights came on, an indication that we must fasten our seat belts. Even in my distress I almost laughed out loud, thinking of what had happened two days earlier.

We were leaving by plane then, too, from Atlanta for New Orleans. Howard's mother and father had brought us to the airport and were waiting to wave good-bye. The crackling of the radio between tower and cockpit could be heard.

I was idly perusing the various signs posted on the walls

when one bit of public relations made a bid for my undivided attention: "This cabin is pressurized for your greater comfort and safety." I thought of the fact that luggage compartments are sometimes nonpressurized and sat straight up in my seat.

"Howard! Do you remember that pressure-packed can of soil sterilizer we put in the big bag?" He looked up from his book and nodded.

"What will happen to it if the compartment isn't pressurized? Isn't there some possibility it could explode?"

He thought a moment and then answered, "I don't think so. But I guess it won't hurt to ask." He motioned for the stewardess.

Ghastly visions of holes being blown in the side of the plane and a fatal plunge to the ground made me wish I had never heard of soil sterilization. We had been told that some of the vegetables grown in Costa Rica were dangerous to eat without first treating them in a solution of iodine or chlorine. I wasn't at all surprised when the further comment was made that this took something out of the flavor. In fact, I had a sneaking suspicion it would add something. So, we had entertained grand thoughts of our own little sterile garden with hygenic lettuce and celery and strawberries.

The pretty young lady leaned over our seat and with a nice smile said, "Yes, sir, may I help you?"

Howard grinned lopsidedly. "I hate to bother you and I know it's silly . . . and I'm sure there's no cause for concern, but . . ."

Her smile tightened a little as she interrupted him. "Why don't you just tell me, anyway."

He straightened his necktie and plunged on. "We packed a can of soil sterilizer in one of our bags. And it's a pressure-pack and I just wondered, that is my wife wondered, if it could possibly explode if the luggage compartment isn't pressurized?" He didn't quite meet my outraged glare as he quickly continued. "I don't think it could damage the plane or anything like that, but I'm not sure whether the gas could possibly leak into the passenger space or not, and the instructions are pretty definite about avoiding breathing and contact with the skin and all that." His voice trailed off, and I froze in my seat when the stewardess, instead of reassuring us that there was no danger or even taking time to reply, simply scuttled into the pilots' section. The plane stopped taxiing immediately. I gulped and looked at Howard. He just slumped lower in his seat.

When the captain stepped through the small door into the forward section where we were sitting, I had an insane desire to yell, "I'm innocent. I didn't do it!" This is a carryover from my childhood, when, after doing something undesirable, I would burst into tears on seeing my mother or father and say, "I didn't do it." "It" was usually unknown to them, but within a matter of minutes I would tell all. Only this time I didn't want to tell anything.

He came straight to our seat, leaned over and asked quietly, "What kind of can did you say that was?"

With the man's face only inches away from his, Howard found it difficult to open his mouth. "A can of stoil serilizer," he spoonerized. Then, regaining his composure, he delved into his briefcase and came up with the folder presented with the can when it was purchased. "I planned to read more about it on the flight," he finished lamely.

The pilot nodded, ducked back into his domain, and we began what seemed an hour-long wait. Since the captain had taken the folder with him, we didn't have even the opportunity to pass the time in research. At about the time we were ready to pass on from knuckle-cracking to nail-chewing, the tempo of the motors picked up, and we began once again to taxi. Howard said, "Well, back to terminal."

Then we realized that we were on the runway, gaining speed for the takeoff. Just after we lifted into the air, the stewardess reappeared and stopped at our seat. "Thank you for giving us that information. The tower feels there is no danger of the can exploding . . ." I heaved a deep sigh of relief. ". . . But should it do so," she continued, "the pilot will know what it is and can act accordingly." She showed her even white teeth in an imitation of a smile and continued on her way.

We sat stiffly and as lightly as we could for the next two hours and fifteen minutes and had only one really bad moment. Whether due to freak atmospheric conditions or the air conditioning system, a thin, white vapor gushed gently from the ventilation registers along the aisle until the aisle itself was ankle-deep in the fog. We both stared in fascination until it completely disappeared a few minutes later. Neither of us had the nerve to ask the stewardess what it was. I, for one, experienced great relief when we landed at the International Airport in New Orleans.

I gave a surreptitious look around me as we left the plane. I didn't see any sign of the gaping hole I half expected to find. I don't know what a Jet-Prop costs, but I imagined it would be a trifle more than I could save for out of the grocery money. All I wanted to do in that moment was to get out without causing any more trouble and to be just as inconspicuous as possible.

We had stepped off into a blustery, rainy afternoon. When I peered around to look at the plane, my taffeta cartwheel sailed off my head and bounced along on its rim under the jet next to us and down toward the hangers.

One of the airport attendants waiting with umbrellas for the passengers took off in a sprint after the hat. I almost snatched off my high heels and joined him in the chase when I saw the pilot, copilot, and stewardesses start down the ramp.

They were just in time to see the young man return, his clothes a soaking mess, to hand me my wet and battered facsimile of a hat. I apologized profusely and thanked him as I tried to hide under the umbrella. I didn't have to see the head-shaking as the crew passed me—I felt it.

My intrepid husband and two daughters had just disappeared into the terminal. He declared later that they thought I was just behind them; but I didn't blame them at all, especially when one of the stewardesses threw this consolation over her shoulder: "Don't look so glum. These trips get pretty dull sometimes when everything goes smoothly."

And here we were, two days later, in a similar situation. We would have to make the plane stop its takeoff maneuvers and let us off. I wondered if they would look upon it as relieving the monotony of routine.

Howard reached across me to push the buzzer when Karen looked up from her coloring and asked, "What are passports, Mommy?"

I was watching for the pleasant, accommodating young lady to appear and answered, "The little green books with our pictures in them, Honey." I almost missed her next remark in my concern that the stewardess wouldn't get there fast enough to get us off the plane.

"Oh. I have 'dose in my bag. I like the pictures."

Howard and I both made a grab for the black plastic bag with KAREN printed in gold on the side. It looks much like a hatbag and can hold a great quantity of things. Now colors, booklets, jackstones, pieces of puzzles, doll clothes and two hundred and eighty-five other things tumbled onto the seats and out into the aisle.

There they were—on the top of the pile. And the plane left the ground with the Stevens family intact.

We flew out across the Gulf of Mexico, high above the fluffy cumulus clouds of late summer. There were several hours of smooth flying over water, and then the plane began to cut across the small Central American countries. Our first stop was in Guatemala City, Guatemala. I couldn't even see the airport, and when we swooped down past the craggy mountains to land I changed my idea of the expression "landing on a dime." It wasn't just an expression!

I considered the advantages of overland travel, even if it does take weeks. By the time we had made a few more stops, equally hair-raising, I vowed to walk home if it were necessary.

At each airport in Guatemala, El Salvador, Honduras, and Nicaragua, we had the dubious honor of being sprayed for any insects we might be harboring. The scene was the same each time. As the plane began to approach the terminal, the stewardess would come down the aisle with a spray can of insecticide, pointing and pushing the button in the general direction of each passenger.

The first time it happened Karen looked up and around at the sound just in time to get the full benefit on the lower half of her face instead of the back of her head. She made a horrible face and started spluttering and wiping off her mouth with her hand. "Whew-ee, Daddy, is *that* what they drink here?"

Since we didn't have visas to visit any of the countries

where we stopped, we weren't allowed to get off the plane. It was stifling in the cabin. After being thoroughly doused with insecticide our sense of smell was murdered long before the end of our journey. It was sometime before we connected the the spray with the odd phenomena of people discretely edging away from us or maneuvering to stand upwind.

Finally we were off on the last portion of the trip. The flight between Nicaragua and Costa Rica was to be a short one, and all of us were tired. The children had played together up and down the aisles, and we had used the eight hours to become better acquainted with some of our fellow missionaries. Then the weather began to get rough, and the seat belt light stayed on causing all of us to settle down in our respective locations.

We were about an hour late arriving over San Jose. The clouds were so thick that, in looking out the window, I could not see the tip of the wing through the swirling mist. We began circling the airport at a steep angle. This airport, too, is surrounded by mountains. Suddenly it became too much for me and I put my head down on the arm, disregarding my already battered hat.

The monotonous circling was broken by the plaintive plea of a small boy behind us. "But, Mother, I *have* to!" His mother argued, tried to get his mind channeled in another direction, and finally obtained permission from the stewardess for them to leave their seats.

They had been gone only a few minutes when the plane was hit by a bolt of lightning. We had been aware of thunder for a short time and had tried not to dwell on the possibility of being in the center of the storm. The big plane yawed, dropped several hundred feet, straightened out, and was back on its pattern over the airport in a matter of seconds.

I had forgotten David and his mother but looked up to see them weaving their way down the aisle, fighting to stay on their feet. The child's eyes were large in a face almost devoid of color. His mother was slightly pale, too, and when they were resettled in their seats she leaned around to say, "That's probably the last knob he'll ever push as long as he lives!"

I said, "What happened?"

She laughed. "He was pushing and pulling every knob and handle he could find in the bathroom. I was trying to make him hurry so I said, 'David, stop that. You might push the wrong one.' He looked at me out of the corner of his eye and jabbed another one. Then the floor dropped out from under us and we frantically had to grab on to the handrails. Now he thinks he caused it."

The ground felt good under my feet. Everything looked wonderful, and even though we were suffering a little from the wrench of leaving country and home, we were happy to be there.

To our delight we heard some yells from the upper balcony of the terminal and saw a huge banner proclaiming, "Welcome, Southern Baptists!" All the students already underway with their studies and the resident missionaries were there to meet us.

I stopped right in the middle of a puddle and looked up to wave at people and banner. Suddenly a feeling of inadequacy threatened to overcome me. I wondered how many wrong buttons I would push, how many bad decisions I would make in the year ahead.

Chapter 2

The men in the customs division were polite. They were even kind. And this first barrier dissolved almost magically before us. This was not always to be so in our comings and goings, but we were grateful that they did not question us too closely that day.

They took one horrified look at my bulging bag and waved me and the children on into the waiting room. It was just as well. It would have created a permanent bottleneck had we been called upon to dump the contents of our three catchalls on their counters. We were teasingly accused of having bribed the men to let us through the line since everyone else had to take his turn and be inspected. I thought it was the other way around. I believe they would have bribed us if we had insisted on being checked.

After a considerable wait everyone got through customs and collected his passport. We climbed aboard the bus with all those who had met us and started for town. It was a long ride, and I found it hard to concentrate on all the conversations going on inside of the bus and to see all of the things we were passing at the same time.

The Spanish Language School has a system called "big brothers." Each family already in school takes the responsibility for one of the families coming in. They find a house or an apartment, look for a maid, buy groceries, and get the house in order. Then they enrol the parents in Language School and the children in school or kindergarten. It is an antidote to weary bones and confused minds to find everything done upon arrival.

Our big brother and sister, Wilson and Martha Donehoo, had taken good care of us, and Martha sat beside me on the bus explaining about the maid and house. "We had to change houses. You know we sent you a description of one." I nodded. "We had to change that one, but I hope you'll like the one we have for you."

I said, "Martha, if its got enough bed space for the four of us and a door to close, it will be enough and more tonight." She laughed. "I mean it. I won't fuss about a thing."

She said, "I hope you keep feeling that way! Oh, you're to eat dinner with us tonight if that's all right."

"Anything will be fine," I mumbled. I was afraid I was going to fall asleep before we got there. We unloaded family after family until we were almost the last ones off the bus. As we walked into the house, I had a confused impression of picture windows with no drapes and a small front terrace—a complete lack of privacy.

The maid met us and Wilson introduced her. I blurted out in English, "I'm glad you're going to work for us." He translated, and she beamingly took our bags into the bedroom.

I looked at the windows. There were only about three feet between the front of the house and the sidewalk. It was beginning to get dark so I switched on the lights, and people passing by looked in curiously. I turned to our big brother. "Wilson, I said I wouldn't fuss about a thing, but do you have a suggestion as to how we can sleep in here? I believe we'd create a scandal."

He scratched his head and said, "I'll talk to the landlord. He lives upstairs."

When he came back shortly all he told us was, "Well, we'll see. Are you ready to eat"?

We followed him down the street. I hadn't had time to unearth any flat-heeled shoes, so I rocked along on cobblestones, smooth pavement, dirt paths, and more cobblestone, finally reaching the house several blocks away.

Dinner was delicious. We sat and talked for a while until I noticed the girls almost falling out of their chairs. Wilson walked us back home. I don't know who was more relieved to see brand-new drapes covering the window, he or I.

"Where do you suppose he got them at this time of the night?" Howard wondered.

Wilson grunted, "Beats me. But I told him to get those windows covered if he had to use a sheet, and that's what I was afraid we'd find."

Our only thoughts then were of bed. We had been awake since 4:00 A.M., and the higher altitude was adding to our state of stupefaction. Karen's, "I want to go to bed, Mommy," almost forced me wide awake. In all her three and one-half years she had never made such a request. Cathy's eyes were completely round, a sign always indicating that within a short time they would close whether she was standing up or lying down.

We didn't take time to look at the house. We just unlocked suitcases and searched for pajamas. Arms and legs were poked into the proper openings, and the little ones were asleep by the time their heads hit the pillows.

I dug through my suitcase, found a gown, and rocked back

on my heels trying to decide about a bath. Wilson had briefed us on the water heater in the bathroom, but in my state of mind I was afraid to try it. It was a Rube Goldberg collection of coils and wires and tubes mounted on the faucets to the shower. The idea was to get in the bathtub, turn on the water, and then flip the switch which would start the water heating as it came through the coils. It was against every safety measure I had ever learned concerning electricity and water, and I was in just enough daze to electrocute myself without half trying.

I discarded the idea of getting clean and headed for bed. Howard went in the same direction, foregoing his usual reading time. We turned out the lamps. With a sigh of relief I sank down to the bed and then just sat there in utter disbelief.

I switched my light back on to be sure I hadn't made a mistake and found my husband patting the bed on his side with the same air of amazement. It did not give a fraction of an inch under our combined weights. Even the floor responded a little when we walked, showing more flexibility than that bed did.

We got back in gingerly and then made a wild grab for each other to keep from sliding right out onto the floor. The slick, well ironed sheet did nothing to dispel the illusion that we were skidding off into space. We felt around cautiously, tried shifting our weight, but nothing happened. We might have been trying to climb into the downy comfort of a marble slab, one that was polished to a high finish and, worse still, one that sloped away from the middle. Finally we settled on an anchor lock with our elbows and with some small feeling of safety drifted off to sleep.

I awoke with a start the next morning and realized that

neither of us had changed positions during the night. I warily pulled my arm loose from his, then wondered if it would remain in that queer, angular position for the rest of my life. Minutes later, normalcy slowly returned.

I eased out of bed, but as soon as I started over the side I knew I was not going to be able to straighten up. I landed on the floor flat on my stomach. My back felt as though I had been doing push-ups all the day before. I called Howard. He awoke, looked around and saw no sign of anyone, so promptly dropped off to sleep again.

"Get me off this floor," I yelled. Our door was partly open into the hall and the maid came running to see if I wanted her. I had said nothing to her beyond the first greeting of the night before and I couldn't explain my predicament now. There I lay sprawled out with one arm crooked in an alarming fashion and bellowed, "Howard!" so sharply he came straight up off the bed.

He still could not see me as I was on the other side of the bed. All he saw was the face of the maid peeking around the door at him. He was so embarrassed that he said, "All right. All right. What do you want?" and grabbed for his robe. He had given up finding his pajamas the night before.

The poor girl fled to the kitchen. We saw little of her during that first day.

My voice was growing feeble, but one last cry brought my husband within viewing range. He stood there and laughed until he bent double. The only thing that saved his neck was the fact that I was as helpless as a baby. When he got over his laughing spree he grabbed me by the shoulders, kneed me in the back and put me on my feet.

I began to splutter indignantly, "If you weren't the father of my children, I'd. . . ." Then he hugged me and said, "Welcome home." And, as always, home was in the security of his arms.

Cathy came yawning out of their bedroom. "Guess what's outside the window?"

She couldn't wait for more than two guesses, both wrong, to tell us, "It's an orange tree and I'm going to climb it."

Karen heard her and came running in. "Me too, me too."

I said, "Don't you think it'd be a good idea to put some clothes on first and eat breakfast? If there is any," I muttered in an aside to Howard.

We unearthed something for them to put on, and about that time our scared maid came to the door and pointed to the dining table. I nodded and got everybody to the table and seated.

Howard said, "Who would like to give thanks this beautiful morning for being in Costa Rica and having a comfortable house and all?"

Karen put up her hand. Then she bowed her head. "'Tank you for all. Amen." We added a deeply felt amen to her short prayer. Breakfast tasted better than I remembered it could. Clean, fresh air was coming in through the open French doors, and we could see the orange tree and little violets in bloom along the edge of a small flower bed.

After breakfast I wanted to inspect the house, and the girls headed outside to climb the tree. Howard went for a closer look at the heating unit, wondering if he could ever get enough hot water for a shave.

The house was small but adequate except for one serious flaw I discovered when I began to unpack. My tour showed two bedrooms and a bathroom, a living room—dining room combination, and a small kitchen. Off the kitchen was the maid's room and bath, and there was even a garage. This was used mostly for drying clothes during the rainy season since we didn't have a car.

I wandered around looking for a while and then got to the onerous task of unpacking. It was then that it dawned on me that except for two small openings in the walls of each bedroom we had no closets. There was room for six or seven dresses in the girls' closet, and I managed to get two of Howard's suits and three of my dresses in ours before I had to start cramming. For weeks we had to live out of suitcases and trunks. A few days before we moved from this house into one a little larger the landlord brought us a clothes rack. In the meantime we almost wore out the same few clothes rather than search through the trunks for something different.

I had to hurry to get things in order before the Donehoos came by for us. We were due at the Spanish Language School at eleven o'clock. I didn't feel very bright, and the subsequent results of this testing we had to undergo showed my feeling to be all too accurate. But by early afternoon we were entered, placed, and almost ready to start. I couldn't begin to imagine what kind of year it would prove to be.

At one time or another during those twelve months I felt like crying as David did, "I sink in deep mire, where there is no standing." At other times I wanted to rejoice, "I will sing of the mercies of the Lord forever."

Chapter 3

I had thought sarsaparilla was something akin to the Mad Hatter's tea, a drink from never-never land. When I was a child this make-believe world was found in the Saturday's movies. Whenever the cowboy sidled up to the bar and ordered "sasparillie" I knew he was the good guy. The villain always demanded straight whiskey.

I learned to my amusement in boning up on Costa Rica before we went that sarsaparilla was listed as one of its main products. It isn't the money producer that coffee or bananas are, but somehow it made that small country more interesting to me.

I had quite a few useless facts such as this tucked away when we arrived in "The Land of Eternal Spring." I knew, for instance, that Costa Rica is a democratic, progressive country. I also discovered that it is smaller than our home state of Georgia. The fact that it has more teachers than soldiers is proudly proclaimed, and we were impressed by all the neat school buildings that we encountered even in the most rural areas.

One of the things I read proved to be very true, but it caused me a lot of trouble after we left Costa Rica. The people are called *Ticos* because they use *tico* or *tica* to form their

24

diminutives; such as *pocotico* for "very little," *momentico* for "just a minute," and so on. Later, I was to be corrected many times by people from other Spanish-speaking countries for using such words.

All the reading we had done beforehand did not prepare us for the beauty of the country, from the wild mountains to the beaches on both the Caribbean and the Pacific. It did not tell us anything about the beauty of the people themselves. The Costa Rican melting pot produces rare attractiveness.

We soon discovered another thing our guide book hadn't mentioned. During the rainy season the afternoon's downpour started at 12:05 each day. If our bus left school a few minutes late we could count on getting thoroughly soaked while dashing the block from the bus stop to our house. The clouds might hang heavy and darken the skies for several hours, but we could set our watches by the beginning of the rain. Curiously enough, it didn't start as a drizzle and build up to a downpour. It began full-blown and usually continued all through the afternoon and the early part of the evening.

An umbrella became an extension of the arm, and one of the first things we had to master was the art of walking down a crowded, narrow sidewalk without putting out anyone's eye and protecting our own at the same time. I never really caught the hang of it, and my husband preferred walking about a half block behind me rather than bear the brunt of the caustic remarks made as I ran the field.

For the first few weeks Howard and I almost forgot why we were in Costa Rica. We were so interested in the multitude of plant materials that we walked around the neighborhood and through the suburbs with our heads stuck in other people's gardens. We blundered off sidewalks and almost walked into cars trying to be polite and look as we strolled past; then we gave up the pretense and just stopped and stared at our leisure.

There seemed to be no particular season for the plants. Azaleas flourished alongside poinsettias; roses bloomed in profusion under great bronze and green and purple orchids hanging from trees whose own clusters of blossoms could be bouquets of daffodils.

Geraniums climbed walls and fences, and one morning Howard clambered up a stone wall, about eight feet high, convinced that the geranium peeking over the top was planted in a pot on a ledge. He got a quick glimpse of the bottom of the plant firmly rooted in the ground about the same time he saw the top of a Great Dane throwing himself at the wall and at Howard's fingers. We accepted eight-foot-tall geraniums as a matter of course from that time on.

An article about Costa Rica was printed in a leading United States magazine during the year that we were there. Its Spanish edition was assigned for outside reading and was widely discussed in several of our classes. One of the photographs showed fence posts that had sprouted new growth. We had laughed over this phenomenon ourselves as we drove through the countryside, but one of my teachers was frankly puzzled.

"Why is it so strange?" he wanted to know. "They're cut from trees after all. So why shouldn't they sprout?"

This logic overcame Howard when I shared it with him. He couldn't help but think of his days as a landscape architect in Nashville, Tennessee, where to plant a tree one pruned the roots, waited a year, balled the roots in burlap, and then planted it with a surgeon's care, fertilizing, filling, and covering the roots with peat moss. Then instructions for watering and feeding as carefully detailed as a baby's formula were left with the new owner. With good luck and good weather, it lived. In Costa Rica the rich soil composed in part of volcanic ash, the mild climate, and the abundant rains cause anything to take root that isn't moved every third day.

This has its drawbacks. Once I failed to recognize a pair of shoes I hadn't worn for a couple of weeks. The dark green suede turned out to be a very prolific mold that had found a happy home on my tan loafers.

The first time we had dinner guests in our home Howard came in with some flowers for the table. I blanched visibly when I saw them; either he had talked someone into giving them to him from their garden or our budget had received a lethal blow for that month. There were several dozen roses, gladiolas, snapdragons, and baby's breath. He finally admitted they all cost about forty cents, and then cheerfully added that he was probably charged about double the regular price being so unlearned in bargaining.

The grass in our yard grew so thick and deeply matted that we bounced on it instead of walking. We wondered how we could cut it without a lawn mower. Then one morning a man appeared at our door to say, "I'm your new gardener."

We must have looked a little nonplussed because he added, "But I'm good. I've had a lot of experience. Of course, I'm so experienced I have to charge more."

Howard asked warily, "How much?"

He said, "Five colones a day," and peered at us to see how we reacted to that amount.

Since it was equal to seventy-five cents, we decided we could afford it and looked around for his lawn mower. I was ready to renege on the deal when he pulled out a long machete and said, "This is my lawn mower."

He must have seen my anguished look because he said,

persuasively, "It does a better job than a lawn mower, I tell you. They just eat the grass up."

The machete was wide and long, hanging from his waist almost to the ground. It had a worn handle, dulled by usage, but the blade was bright and finely honed.

When he started to work, we stopped studying to watch him. He stooped in a half-squat, leveled the machete, and sliced the grass off at a precise height. There was not a blade left standing as the machete swung back and forth in rhythm, and the grass was as smooth and even as velvet.

Howard grunted with each swing the gardener made. I finally queried, "Is it hurting you?"

He said, "Uh-huh! If I tried that I'd plow up the ground or cut off my leg. Probably both."

There was a sense of perfection about the small plot of ground we called a yard when he had finished. He pruned the shrubbery, weeded the flower bed, and trimmed the edges of the lawn. As the sun cast its last light for the day on this tiny bit of green earth, we felt as though we possessed an emerald. The smell of the damp earth and fresh-cut grass added to the delight.

The beauty surrounding us seemed to dispel tiredness at the end of day. The lofty mountains cast long purple shadows across the valleys. "I will lift up mine eyes unto the hills from whence cometh my help," became a refrain of our lives. Even on the days when the rains descended so violently, we were often treated to the sight of a perfect double rainbow in the sky at the close of day.

Chapter 4

The first day of school was a traumatic experience for all of us. As a result of the entrance tests we had been sorted into groups, the members of which were supposed to be at about the same level. I was neither hot nor cold but lukewarm, that is to say about the middle of the heap.

In my group were two Southern Baptists—the other one from Texas—one member of the Church of God from Oregon, a Methodist from Kansas, and an Episcopalian from Texas.

We learned a lot about each other during that term. We were together for all our classes, and the teachers asked a lot of questions like, "Where were you born?" to make us think and use our Spanish. I was ready to cry, "Unfair!" when the question was first asked concerning our birthplace. All the other states were fairly easy to pronounce until it came to Georgia; it had some wild sound like "Hey-or-hee-ah." When I whinnied like a horse, I came close to the pronunciation!

We had been in San Jose several weeks and were well into the program of study when I overheard an interesting conversation. I was sitting at the dining table listening for the 14th time to the tape we had to learn for the next day's assignment. My head was beginning to follow the tape around and around, and I cut it off in disgust.

Karen and Jill, another M.K. (Missionary Kid), were playing in the patio. Sounds drifted in through the open French doors. Karen said, in a rather offhand manner, "My mommy and daddy go to school."

Jill, who was her elder by a year, took her down a peg. "I know it, stoopid. So do mine."

Karen remonstrated. "They're too old. School is for 'lil kids."

Jill scoffed, "Oh, no it's not." Then she added in a curious tone, "Don't you know what missionaries do?"

Karen said, with all confidence, "Yeah!" There was a pause. "What?"

Jill said, "They go to school, that's what. Come on let's climb that tree."

I eavesdropped shamelessly. School was all Jill had known for her parents as they had come almost directly from seminary to language school. We had finished seminary when Karen was a year old, so school for mommy and daddy was another new experience for her.

Howard laughed when I told him. "I'm afraid I agree with her. I am too old."

Both of us used that excuse as a crutch in the weeks following. We were continually on the lookout for a new scapegoat, but there weren't many to be found. We couldn't blame our difficulties with the language on the school. It is under the auspices of the Commission on Ecumenical Missions and Relations of the United Presbyterian Church in the U. S. A. and is used by almost all the boards, agencies, and sending bodies in the States to train their missionaries before they go into the Spanish-speaking countries of the world.

The Spanish Language School was founded in 1942 in Medellín, Colombia. In 1950 the school moved to San Jose because of the more tolerant attitude toward Protestants. Since it was founded, the school has trained several thousand missionaries from more than 130 different groups.

We couldn't blame the up-to-date teaching methods nor the competent teachers, either. The course of study is based on the idea that language learning should start with hearing, then speaking, and at last to reading and writing. So no English was used in the classrooms, and we stumbled along.

We studied, attended classes, and groped our way through the maze of everyday living. We had tests, exams, recitations, and moved from one class to another. Someone was probably seeing some growth in me, but I failed to see it. I had difficulty understanding how saying "The dog is brown" without making more than four mistakes would ever make me bilingual.

After weeks of study our class was conducted along these lines: "What is this?" "That is a pencil." "What color is the pencil?" "The pencil is red." It humiliated me to realize this was the hardest work I had ever done in any school.

My favorite teacher drilled us constantly. We recited as a group and we recited as individuals. He started each day with a big smile and a confident air. It was distressing to see the glum look that settled deeper into his finely molded Latin features as the hour wore on.

He was polite though. He didn't go into laughing fits as my first period teacher did everytime I tried to repeat her words. Nor did he groan and tug at his moustache as my fourth period instructor did each day. I was getting some deep-seated guilt feelings about that moustache. This little bit of hair on the lip is a status symbol, a way of life, an indication of masculinity. Now my abuse of his language was about to cause him to pull it out, hair by hard-grown hair.

One day in class I was musing over the bitter thorn in the flesh I was turning into, for all my teachers, when a direct question brought me back into focus. "Señora, dígame, por favor, qué es ésto?"

He was pointing at his nose, and I wondered if I could plead mental incompetence. I had no idea what it was. The teacher sighed and said, "Nariz." We chanted, "Nariz," and then began to learn the other parts of the face. I wondered, "Is it possible that they can teach us to speak like adults in a year's time?"

That was to be the job of the Spanish Language School. Its awe-inspiring task is to take men and women from all backgrounds, with staggering varieties of regional accents, vast differences in educational preparation, age ranges of twenty or thirty years, with different capacities and talents for absorbing and using another language, and teach them to work and live in a foreign land.

Our campus was composed of three buildings, two on one side of a broad thoroughfare and one opposite. We were often late if we had to change classes across the street. The cars zipped up and down the streets with the abandonment of four-year-olds free-wheeling on tricycles. And there was the additional obstacle of a railroad spur to cross. The trains glided along the tracks in such silence that a loud warning toot to a pedestrian in the way was liable to cause him to jump straight into the path of an oncoming car or bus.

Many of the classes spilled over into garages, porches, and maintenance buildings. It was distracting to sit with a view of the mountains and the gardens close by. The altitude had a curious effect of exhilaration overlaid with lassitude. The desire to fly with great leaps and bounds over the countryside was tempered with the sobering knowledge that it would take a great effort to lift an index finger to point in the direction one wanted to go. The same combination took a toll in the day's study and concentration.

In retrospect, the first mistake we made when we began talking about fields of service with the Foreign Mission Board was in not asking for assignment to English-speaking work in some part of the world. It is one thing to translate laboriously a passage with dictionary in hand and grammar book available, and another thing to grope through a maze of words thrown at one, wrapped in the paper of emotions and feelings and tied with the bright ribbons of regional accents. The solution is to have an innate ability with another language that transcends mere intelligence or ability to apply one's self to study. But this is a gift, one on the level with singing, and it cannot be bought, borrowed, or stolen.

So I worked out a compromise. It was composed of three basic steps. There were endless variations to this formula, but the three basics satisfied in most cases. When the doorbell rang and I found my ear inundated with sounds I would say, "A little slower, please."

Sometimes this worked, but if I didn't understand the slower version step two went into effect. "Please say it again." More often than not it still sounded like 33 1/3 rpm record playing on 78. Then I would try step three. "Please come back in a short while when my husband will be here." I tried to make this sound very dignified, as if I had understood all along just exactly what the person had been saying, but that such matters would have to be attended to by my husband.

This was usually effective; in fact it was almost guaranteed to leave the person standing at the door or gate with mouth ajar. Especially if it turned out to be, as it did on one occasion, a lady selling cosmetics.

Almost everytime we opened our mouths we made blunders. I couldn't decide whether it was better to act unaware of such *faux pas* or to catch what had been done and apologize. I tended toward the former philosophy as I usually put my foot in deeper when I tried to recover. We were told of a young man, a first term student at the language school, who had this experience; it almost rendered him speechless, with a loss of voice from shock.

He was riding an overcrowded bus from town, holding on to the overhead rod and trying to balance a large, awkward package at the same time. The bus drivers career around corners without attention to the comfort of their passengers. The young man found himself clutching his handhold and shifting weight, frantically trying to keep what little balance he had.

One wild turn undid him completely. Plop! He landed in the lap of a lady sitting nearby. Blushing from head to toe he tried to apologize as he pulled himself up and retrieved his package.

First he said, *"perdóneme"* [Forgive me]. Feeling this was inadequate he tried again. *"Lo siento mucho"* [I'm very sorry].

He was still eliciting nothing but the iciest of glares and he knew he would have to manage something more. So he added, *"Estoy embarazado."* He was attempting to say, "I'm embarrassed," and had reached for a word that was similar to the English. This often works, as many words are almost the same in both languages. But this was not one of those lucky times, and his embarrassment was to increase.

Everyone within hearing distance of the unfortunate man burst out laughing. Even the lady herself managed a smile. It was not until he got home and hurriedly thumbed through his dictionary that he discovered why it was so funny. He had said: "Forgive me. I'm very sorry. I'm pregnant."

Somehow the children made out all right even though they had no such intensive study of the language as their parents did. They had a universal language that seemed to transcend the problems of vocabulary and grammar. This was very gratifying until our own children became more proficient. There was little parental face-saving in having to ask our four-year-old to go and tell the man at the gate what we had been trying to get across to him for several minutes.

There was also another language that leaped over all the problems; the language of love. Even though we made every mistake we could possibly make there still came times when someone would ask, "But you're different; why is this?" Then we had joy in attempting to explain God's love for us and for them.

Karen was so surprised to learn that God speaks Spanish and can understand prayers that are offered in this tongue. She puzzled a long time over this and finally asked, "Did he come to Language School, too?"

Often, people to whom we talked were equally as astonished to realize that God hears and understands them without an interpreter or a go-between. How glad we were to be able to tell them that his is the universal language and that he has a plan for the universe that includes everyone that will hear him.

Chapter 5

Our maid's name was Blanca. She was housekeeper, cook, babysitter, and many other things. For this we paid her about twenty dollars a month. Since we attended classes in the morning and studied in the afternoon, we needed help. With all the aids in the supermarkets in the United States, I could have managed, but in most Latin American countries canned goods are extremely expensive, and frozen foods are practically nonexistent.

There was another, more urgent, reason as well. Stealing is the major crime in San Jose, and we were urged not to leave the house unguarded. So Blanca was nightwatchman and guardian of the keys along with all of her other responsibilities.

She spoke no English, and I knew little Spanish; this hindered things in the beginning. But she loved to talk, and as long as I nodded my head from time to time, the deluge of words would continue. The fact that I seldom had much knowledge of what she was talking about didn't seem too important to her.

We soon established certain routines and began the habit of eating supper early each day. One afternoon Howard went to town and didn't appear at the usual hour to eat. Somehow I got the message across to her that we would wait for him.

I was surprised to hear some loud weeping sounds from the kitchen a few moments later. I rushed in anxiously. "What is the matter, Blanca?"

She snuffled once or twice, wiped her sleeve over her eyes and wailed, "My supper is ruined." Then she burst into tears again.

Looking around the kitchen to see what we were having for supper that would spoil so rapidly, I saw frankfurters in a pan, buns on a tray, fruit salad in a bowl, and a package of potato chips still to be opened. My laugh threatened to bubble over as I said, "Blanca, I believe it will be all right."

Good maids were hard to find, and even the most dependable ones seemed to tire of routine and the security of working for the same family very long. If a little upset didn't occur to give them an excuse to leave, they would often precipitate a crisis. I was afraid that's what was happening. We eased around the house carefully that evening and were all at the table early the next morning for breakfast.

Blanca bounced in smiling at everybody. "Good morning. Isn't it a beautiful day!" she chirped. She sang her way back into the kitchen as we sat glued to our chairs in amazement.

She continued to be happy and worked her long hours without complaint. However, when we brought home a small puppy for Karen this mood changed. Our youngest daughter loves animals of all kinds, and we hoped that it would be a companion for her during the time we had to be away from home each day.

Blanca did not share Karen's love of animals. She seized the first opportunity to drop a bit of advice. "Señora, I don't think that puppy is good for Karen."

"Why?" I asked as I began to look for mange or fleas.

"Oh, it's just not good for little girls to play with dogs." This was her reply, and she would not budge from it nor explain it. We finally shrugged it off as superstition and forgot it.

Blanca didn't forget. A day or so later she said to Howard, "Señor, that dog is going to be a huge one when he grows up. As big as a horse!" she added ominously.

We looked at the puppy's paws, and Howard agreed drily that when he matured, he might be on the large side but he doubted his getting as big as a horse.

Blanca didn't say anything else that day, but the battle to get rid of the dog soon swung into full force. The next day I heard a shriek and ran to find her up on a chair swatting at the dog with her wet mop. The puppy was running around the chair chasing his tail, and everytime he reached the front she added to the momentum by slapping his backsides.

When she saw me she stopped hitting at him and cried, "He chased me all the way from the bedroom." I could visualize the chasing. The little fellow loved to play. Whenever we went for a walk, he ran in and out between our legs, trying to get us to run and play with him. But in the puppy's playfulness, Blanca saw only viciousness.

One Friday weeks later Blanca approached me with, "Doña Norma, my brother is a good man." I nodded and waited for her to enlarge on her statement. She didn't say anything else and seemed to be waiting for me to say something so I obliged with, "That's good."

She seemed to be satisfied and added, "He likes animals." Again the pause and I said, "Well, that's good too."

She turned and left the room as I stared at her retreating back and tried to make some sense out of the conversation. Little by little the light dawned. We were still being warred upon, and the next phase was direct assault. She brought her brother by to meet us. Following the introductions and some polite exchange she said, "He would like to have a dog so much."

Then her eyes lit up as though the thought were born in that moment. "Oh, wouldn't it be wonderful if he could take the little dog. He has so much room out in the country, and the sweet little animal could play out of doors all day, and they would feed him good and look after him and. . . ."

On and on it ran. My eyes were glazing over trying to keep track of so many words and so much praise for the dog. Then she added the clincher: "You'll have to leave in a few months, and you won't be able to take him with you. Wouldn't it be better to give him away now before Karen gets too attached to him?"

Of course we had taken that into consideration when we bought the puppy. We had explained it to Karen, but a three-year-old going on four might make a promise one day and forget it the next. It was asking a lot of her, but I came to the conclusion I had been bettered in the battle. I made a feeble compromise. "If it's all right with Karen and won't make her too unhappy, he can have the dog."

Evidently Blanca was at her persuasive best with our offspring because Karen happily volunteered to give the puppy up, adding, to our chagrin: "It's okay. I like cats better anyway."

She was using English, or I'm sure that Blanca would have started her strategy immediately against cats, generally and specifically.

This *Tica* found it very easy to express her emotions. Even the children were fascinated by her ability to switch from one extreme to another. They seemed to understand that she wasn't always unhappy when she cried nor sincerely happy when she laughed. She used emotions much as another person might use words, merely as more ornate vehicles for her feelings.

Blanca was a delightful person, above the average in education and social background of most of the maids in Costa Rica. Her father had been a doctor but was killed in the revolution that took place in 1948. Her mother had been left with several children and no means of support, so the older girls began working as maids when they were still in their teens. She used good grammar, could play the piano a little, had many friends among the upper class, successfully hiding from them her occupation, and was conscious of good etiquette in all phases of living.

She excelled in cooking and enjoyed the dinner guests we had from time to time. Usually the menu was left to her discretion, but on one ocasion she approached me with, "Would it be possible to spend a little more for the meat this time? I'd like to buy something special." This uncommon request intrigued me.

I gave her permission. We were expecting our little brother and sister, Guy and Judy Williamson, to eat with us after their arrival. Her sister, Marina, was going to work for them, and since she was a good cook too, they often competed with one another on a friendly basis. I was startled, however, to discover that she had spent about five times the usual amount for meat. She told me what she had bought, but I was still on unfamiliar ground concerning the Spanish names for the different cuts of meat.

The day of the dinner she blustered around with more importance than usual and seemed uncommonly nervous over the preparation of the meal. At two o'clock she came upstairs to ask me, "Do you want me to carve the meat in the kitchen, or can you carve it at the table tonight?"

Still unsure of what was involved I answered, "Whatever you think best."

All afternoon she fluctuated between the two solutions and ran upstairs to tell me each time she changed her mind. I think she feared I didn't have the savoir faire to cope with such an elite piece of meat. "Elite" was the word she used in her description of it and a rather formidable picture was forming in my thinking. Her nervousness was catching, and I approached the dinner hour as jumpy as she was.

At five o'clock she made up her mind once again that the meat would be more resplendant if she brought it in its entirety to the table and I carved it. Then she proceeded to outline carefully for me the exact manner in which to cut and serve it. At six o'clock, thirty minutes before the guests were due, she reversed her decision. Then, as we sat down to eat, she whispered to me that she was going to let me do it after all.

I squirmed nervously and hoped I wouldn't miff my one and only chance. Blanca brought in the vegetables: rice, green beans, *ayote* and the huge salad platter—her own speciality of a halved pineapple filled with cubes of pineapple, bananas, and oranges in a cooked dressing with whipped cream. The platter was garnished with other fruit and took up a third of the space on the table. Then came two long loaves of freshly made bread sprinkled with cheese.

At long last she came in bearing a huge platter that she had borrowed from a neighbor, holding an enormous piece of meat. Heralds with trumpets announcing her coming would not have been out of place.

I had to breathe deeply to stop the merriment that threatened to overwhelm me. She went back into the kitchen, and I stuffed my napkin in my mouth while everyone stared at me.

Sitting on the table, ready to be carved, was a pork backbone.

It was delicious, and recognizing that pork cost several times more than the best beef steak or roast, we knew that it was an elite piece of meat to her. She seemed relieved to find that I had been able to handle the carving. I couldn't explain to her that even the residents of Catfish Row in Georgia could have acquitted themselves admirably with that bit of meat.

Blanca was Catholic by birth and she remained Catholic. If she could have gotten past her social awareness, we might have had more success in helping her to see religion as a personal experience. She visited an evangelical church once or twice, but came away convinced that only the poorest class of people attended, and she was uncomfortable with them.

Blanca asked questions from time to time about the differences in our religion. She showed a greater awareness of God than many people with whom we talked. But half-truths are often more difficult to get past than complete ignorance, and she had a storehouse of truths and falsehoods all scrambled together. It was discouraging to live with her a year and have to leave without the conviction that she knew Christ and loved him. But we remembered Jesus words: "And herein is that saying true, One soweth and another reapeth" (John 4:37). We could only pray that the seed had been sown.

Chapter 6

The word *paseo* became a familiar one with pleasant connotations for us. It means "a walk" or "a stroll" literally, but it can also mean "an outing." The Language School had one for the students every few weeks, and a most memorable one was our trip to the Volcano Poas. It is necessary to be at the rim of the volcano by daybreak in order to see its crater and mouth.

We crept out of the house in the dark of an early spring morning and met the others at the school to make the trip. There was no light in the sky when we climbed out of the bus and struck out up the steep path. The wind blew against us, and I was bent double trying to accommodate my body to the slope and not be keeled over by the wind.

The cold air and altitude plus the unaccustomed exercise had me panting in seconds. Soon my heart started pounding violently, and before I had staggered upwards 500 yards I was envisioning a heart attack, my family weeping over my poor, inert body and . . . and then I stopped. My poor, inert body was being shuffled from one official to another as miles of red tape tangled around my ears. I couldn't resolve the dilemma, so I took a deep breath of the chilly air and struggled on.

Howard was having little trouble with the incline and teased me about being a poor hillbilly. I didn't even bother to answer him, but that was from a lack of breath, not for want of an adequate retort.

The sky didn't seem to get any lighter; it just seemed less dark after awhile, and we were able to make out trees and bushes along the side of the rocky road. Then we were walking in semidarkness, marveling at the difference in the terrain. For long stretches we climbed through dense forests and then through open meadows with the mists swirling around rocks and stunted trees. I was glad we were surrounded by people.

At one point we rounded a curve and lost sight of the road as it disappeared into a towering forest. There were coniferous evergreens of such height that the little light we had was blocked. The ground was thick with needles, and fallen limbs were covered with deep, green moss. The silence was a physical thing. Howard and I stopped and soon found ourselves alone. The words from *Evangeline* came to both of us at the same time: "This is the forest primeval." It seemed untouched by the ages.

We went on and I began fussing, "Six miles, my foot! It's more like twelve. I can't walk another step! Nothing is worth all this to see!"

Howard just laughed, grabbed my arm, and ran with me a short distance to a huge boulder by the side of the road. A few minutes rest made me eager to start again, and we speeded up hoping to reach the top before sunrise.

Then we rounded the last bend in the road, climbed the slope, and picked our way around huge rocks to the rim of the volcano. The sun peeked up over the mountains and lit up the crater, but the far rim was still hazy in the distance. The clouds were turned into golden heaps of froth, and the light sparkled and leaped and bounced back and forth off the rocks in the crater like echoes. We looked and looked, unconscious at the moment of the fact that we were colder than we had ever been in all our lives.

Inside the crater was a mound that appeared to be the mouth from which steam escaped. It gasped and snorted into the open air. Someone, with more hunger of body than soul of a poet, said, "Wow! It looks like a great big doughnut over a steaming cup of coffee." About that time the sun went behind the clouds, and the spell was broken.

Several small fires were started, and we all brought out bags of food. The cold chicken and ham sandwiches made the best breakfast possible. Hot coffee and chocolate helped to warm us a little. Then someone shouted, "Hey, look at those nuts!"

We rushed to the edge of the crater and looked down to see two of the men deep into the volcano working their way down toward the fissure. One of the men yelled at them, but his voice didn't carry that far. I gulped and moved back a few inches. I knew it was a long way down, but until I had seen the two tiny dots moving along I hadn't fully grasped the distances.

One of the dots turned and looked back, and the leader of the group made great sweeping motions with his arms, trying to indicate to them to return immediately. The man caught up with his companion and pointed back up. They started in our direction, but the volcanic ash that had allowed them a fairly rapid descent gave way beneath them, and they slid back almost as far as they climbed each time. They slipped and slid until they reached the upper part where the ground was firmer.

Howard, Bill Gray, and I started back down, confident that our going down would be easier than the climb up. We trotted along for awhile; then far below us we could see the road make a long swing to the right before it cut sharply back to the left. Somebody made the suggestion that we take a shortcut across the meadow and intersect the road. I should have known better. Shortcuts have always been disastrous for me, but this one seemed a cinch. We were bound to reach the road shortly, and the meadow looked a lot more inviting than the road did. We loped along at a good pace, over grass, around fallen trees, up one cliff we had not seen from the distance, and down and up a deep ditch. But we were still sure of seeing the road at any moment and beating everybody else to the bus.

After the third deep ditch we had clambered in and out of, things got quiet. We were having enough trouble staying on our feet. When we slid down a steep embankment and found ourselves at the bottom of a future Grand Canyon, we decided to walk at the bottom of it instead of climb the other side. Our only consolation was the fact that we were still going downhill. Reason told us we'd have to come out sooner or later. But reason didn't help our sore feet and aching muscles.

We walked for miles and still no road. It had gotten funny by that time instead of tragic, and we were staggering down the mountainside like idiots when we almost lurched into the back door of a farmhouse built into the side of the hill. We ran around the side of the house and saw the road below us. In single file we loped down the rutted driveway, scattering chickens and geese in our path and hoping the bus had not left us. We reached the road and looked. It was completely bare.

Then Bill shouted, "There it is!" and pointed above us. We had come out about a quarter of a mile below it. I refused to budge an inch until both men pointed out to me that I was going to have a hard time explaining how I got there if the bus had to stop and pick me up. So I climbed with them, muttering the whole way.

I pulled myself into the bus and collapsed in my seat. Even the surprised remarks of the others on finding us there didn't help. I just huddled in my corner and longed for home.

The bus took us to our corner. Howard got off first, then reached up to give me a hand. Nothing moved. I was so sore I couldn't get a foot in front of me. Howard said, "Bill, give her a push." So with me protesting in a loud voice, Bill pushed and Howard pulled, and they got me down to the sidewalk.

They thought I was being too dramatic, so each man seized an arm and started off down the street with me at a fast lope. I was yelling at the top of my lungs by that time. "Let me down, you lunatics! You're killing me!"

This only spurred them on, and we made the entire block with my feet in the air half the time and dragging behind me the other half. They ran gaily up the flight of steps to the front door and deposited me on the landing.

Our maid opened the door, and Cathy and Karen, still pajama-clad, greeted me with, "Where you been? What's the matter, Mommy?"

I said, "Nothing is the matter," as I crawled in on all fours through the door.

I said, "Why do you think something is the matter?" as I climbed the stairs on my hands and knees.

I said, "I think I'm dying," as I pulled myself into the shower, still on all fours.

Chapter 7

"Mommy, make them talk right!" The wail came from Karen. I listened to hear what Cathy and Fabrienne were saying. There was an animated conversation going on as the two girls played dolls. Cathy was chattering away in English and Fabrienne was jabbering in French. Then they would switch over to Spanish. It was nothing new. I could sympathize with Karen though, for it was hard for me to catch even a drift of what they were saying.

Fabrienne was our little next-door neighbor from France. The two girls often played together until Gallic temperament and American independence would split them up temporarily. Today they were happy, but since Karen felt left out I put on her sweater and we went for a walk.

I thought about our daughters as we walked along. They had had more adjustments to make than we and had taken most of it in stride. But they were so different. While languages came naturally to Cathy, Karen was almost as lost as I. Cathy had friends from Germany, France, and China, as well as those from Costa Rica, and strange sounding words flew in all directions when they played together. Yet, they all seemed to understand.

One day I asked Cathy, "Do you mean to tell me, when

you're speaking English and Fabrienne is using French, that you understand each other?"

She looked at me coolly. "Of course!" So I quietly envied her ability and tried to keep things running smoothly for a little sister who was in the dark, too.

That afternoon we walked slowly, looking at the flowers and greeting all the dogs and cats we met. In Karen's love for animals she had an undeniable communication with them. I have often felt like climbing the nearest tree on meeting a horse-sized dog, then he would grovel in the dust at Karen's feet. She was a small, fragile child with soft brown curls hanging to her waist. It was a heart-stopping sight to watch a great beast bound up to her looking as though he could swallow her in two or three bites, then to see him roll over on his back to be petted.

As we strolled along in our walks, someone usually came out and tried to make friends with Karen as we passed our neighbors' houses. She was shy, and when this happened she would hold her arms up to me to take her, then duck her head under my chin in spite of all the talking and cajoling. But if a kitten or puppy should come out of a house, our shy one would be down in a streak, running around the yard like a wild Indian.

After we left the house that day, one of our neighbors did her best to get Karen to say hello to her. But she pulled her bashful act. About that time Cathy and Fabrienne came flying out the front door, down the steps, and past us, yelling something.

"Cathy, where are you going?" I called.

She came to a skidding halt and doubled back. "We're going to the store to get some glue. Daddy said we could. Oh, hello, Señora. How are you? Please excuse me." And she sprinted off to catch up with Fabrienne. Her manners were usually deplorable, so I was proud of that brief bit of courtesy. The girls were a study in contrasts. Cathy was snaggle-toothed, and her face was made up mostly of enormous eyes that changed with every mood. Karen almost always looked as though I had just dressed her and combed her hair.

The lady looked at me. "Is she yours, too?"

I nodded. She shook head. "You just have two?" I nodded again.

She said, "Well, all the difference went into them." It was a cryptic remark, but after thinking about it I realized that she meant that all the differences to be found between brothers and sisters in a large family seemed to have gone into our two.

She was right. Cathy seldom met a stranger, and Karen had to work her way carefully into relationships with others. Cathy played and fussed and made up and fought again. Her little sister never quarreled with anyone. She was a "mother" to the younger children and peacemaker with her contemporaries. A common joke among new acquaintances of ours was, upon looking over both girls, to say, "Which one is adopted?"

Cathy looked forward to school each day; Karen hated nursery school. We tried taking her to the one sponsored by the Spanish Language School, but each morning was a trial, having to talk brightly about "playing with your friends," and so on. Then the little neighborhood kindergarten was worked out, and she seemed to enjoy going there two hours a day. After that she was ready to be through with school.

We had looked forward to Christmas. For two weeks we were freed from classes, and the town was festive. One night we took the girls downtown to see the little shops that had sprung up around the plaza. It reminded me of a county fair with small booths displaying toys, Christmas ornaments, food, and gifts. Lights were strung from the jerry-built shops, and people flowed around the block, looking, bargaining, and buying. We gave the children a couple of *colones* apiece to spend, and I thought we were going to set a new record for the number of trips we made all the way around before they decided what to buy. Their choices were typical. Cathy bought some candy that she particularly enjoyed. Karen squatted down on her heels in front of a large wooden container full of tiny little figures, finally realizing that she could buy one of each of the animals and people and still have a few *centavos* left over. She was enchanted with anything tiny—dolls, furniture, miniatures of any kind. These crudely made little representations of the nativity provided her with hours of enjoyment.

Christmas was on Sunday. We got up early to have our presents and eat breakfast before leaving for Sunday School and church. The major gift for the children was a folding wooden doll house and furniture that we had brought with us from the States and had hidden away for Christmas. Each of them had smaller presents, but the doll house was the main attraction. Karen had played with it for awhile when she said, "Oh, I want to put *my* dolls in."

For a moment we didn't know what she was talking about, then realized that she meant Mary and Joseph and the animals. I said, "Well, go and get them. I suppose they'll fit in pretty well for Christmas morning."

She started up the stairs and then said, "But I can't. Blanca put them up on the high shelf."

Howard came to the rescue. "Come on and show me where they are." And they ran up the stairs hand in hand.

When they started back down he was still carrying her, having picked her up to reach the top shelf for her figures. He was wearing knitted bedroom slippers, and as he reached the landing and started on down, they skidded on the terrazzo steps. He slid down the stairs on his back, trying to hold Karen up to keep her from being hurt.

He almost succeeded. Her right foot was somehow caught beneath him. She didn't cry long but would not put any weight on the foot. When I tried massaging it, she screamed.

I looked at Howard. "Do you suppose we can find a doctor? I hate to disturb anyone on Christmas."

He thought a minute, then mentioned the doctor we knew best. "He said he was taking the family out of town for the holidays. It's the only way he can get a rest."

One of our fellow missionaries was a doctor and a good one. Wilbur and Gladys Lewis were studying Spanish, expecting to go to Paraguay and work in the hospital there. But, on checking the time, we realized that they had probably left for their church. Then Howard said, "There is that doctor who lives next door to the Turners. Since it isn't too far, it wouldn't take me but a few minutes to see if he would be willing to have a look at her foot."

He was back with the doctor in about thirty minutes. The young, clean-cut man impressed us both with his easy manner with Karen, and we were very relieved that he had done his training in the United States and had a good command of the English language. After some probing he nodded. "Un-huh. I believe we'd better take this little lady down to the hospital and get it x-rayed. There may be a broken bone or two."

He took us in his car. Being with a doctor we cut through some of the usual time-consuming procedures and had only a short wait before the results of the X rays were in hand. He showed them to us, explaining that one of the small bones across the top of the foot was splintered, but little good could be accomplished by putting it in a cast, and since it had not broken the skin there would be no danger of infection. He prescribed a mild sedative for the pain and took us home.

Karen didn't complain of her foot but kept on limping for some time. She looked pale all day and didn't play very much even when the Grays and the Stulls, along with their children, joined us for dinner. By the next morning she was doubled up in pain, not from the foot but from her stomach. Our doctor was still out of town, and since we had called in the other one we checked with him.

He came by the house and after looking her over carefully said, "I think it would be best to have some further X rays made and some blood tests run. I didn't think so yesterday and still have my doubts, but she may have suffered some internal injuries in the fall."

We made the rounds of offices all over town that day. We had to go to two different clinics for X rays, then to a laboratory to make the blood tests. We were to become very familiar with this place in the next few weeks, and our courage, faith, and endurance were to be heavily taxed.

The photographs of her stomach and other organs were normal, but the blood tests showed an exceptionally high eosinophil count. The eosinophils are one of the groups of white blood cells, and a high count usually indicates parasites or an allergy.

Test after test was run looking for amoebas, round worms, pin worms, or anything that would account for it. Nothing was found. Then the doctor said, "We'll put her on an anti-allergy medication and see if it brings the count down. If it does, we can start looking for the culprit."

The following week we were jubilant. The blood test revealed a 100% drop. Our jubilation didn't last long. The next week it was back up higher than before, and she was still taking the medicine.

The doctor sat looking at his reports. He shook his head. "I hate to have to tell you this, but I'm afraid it's very serious. There are three possibilities as far as I can see, and they are all fatal eventually."

I must have stopped breathing. Everything seemed suspended in time. I was listening to the doctor's voice, but something within me was frantically trying to block the words.

He continued. "It could be a very rare form of leukemia. It might be Hodgkin's disease or it could be Addison's disease. I tend toward the latter. She has some other symptoms that are, as yet, almost indiscernable, but I predict that within a few months the more obvious symptoms will appear."

We didn't talk much on the way home, but as soon as we had Karen settled for supper, her father and I left to look for Wilbur Lewis. We had told him about the problem, and he had sympathized with us over the painful blood tests to which Karen was being subjected every week. He and Gladys were just leaving the house when we arrived, but I blurted out the diagnosis the doctor had given us.

Wilbur was silent for a minute, then said rather mildly, "I don't believe it."

He repeated, "I don't believe it, and I'll tell you why. Regardless of what he may have said about the symptoms appearing later, nobody can see that much into the future. If you want me to, I'll get together everything I can find on eosiniphils and come by your house after we get home. Okay?"

Wilbur was confidant, doctor, and friend to all of the missionaries. Called out any time of the day or night, he always came cheerfully. He did not practice medicine in Costa

Rica but worked closely with the doctors at an evangelical hospital in San José. It was not necessary to have a prescription to buy medicine, and he could make suggestions concerning something to alleviate whatever was ailing us.

It was late when he arrived that night, and he had classes early the next day just as we did. But we sat and read and discussed until long past midnight. As he left he made a suggestion. "Would you like for me to talk with the doctor at the hospital about this? I'm not suggesting your doctor is wrong, but he has been a little hasty. I, for one, would like someone else's opinion."

We agreed, and the doctor set up an appointment for us with a good pediatrician. Wilbur went with us to his office, and the man was very frank. "After looking over all the tests and reports and examining Karen, I cannot agree with the diagnosis. I can't say right now what it is, but I can almost assure you without question that it is not one of three possibilities offered you."

He turned to Wilbur. "I'm going to suggest to our friend at the hospital that he have some more tests made for parasites. You know how these tests can be. Sometimes conditions have to be ideal to spot the offender. If the technician leaves a specimen too long before making an analysis, it well may show negative when it should be positive."

Wilbur agreed with him and we left the office feeling relief, although there was still a residue of anxiety that would be a long time clearing up.

We took Karen to the hospital the next day, and the doctor checked her very carefully again. Then he prepared some slides to look for pinworms, although, as he said, this was best done early in the morning. He took the slides himself into the main lab, and we watched as he peered through the microscope. After several minutes he straightened up and shook his head. "This is the first time I've ever felt like giving my right arm to find a worm. Just one would satisfy me!"

Then his face cleared. "But don't worry. We'll come up with something."

The weeks went by. Nothing turned up. Karen's stomach-aches continued, sometimes lasting only a few minutes, at other times hurting for several hours, leaving her pale and drawn.

Then, as suddenly as they had come, they left. She was still having blood tests about once a month, and the erratic white blood cells settled down. The count was still four times higher than it should have been, but they stabilized at that number. The lab work each week was a nightmare for us. Blood had to be taken from her arm, and the little veins were difficult to enter. The first few times she cried. In time, she only turned white around the mouth and didn't say a word nor utter a protest. In a way, this was harder to bear than the crying.

Cathy stood in awe of Karen during these months. Our older one, being the tomboy, was afraid of nothing. That is, nothing, until it came to having injections or her finger pricked for a blood test. Then she bellowed and kicked and threw such fits we finally had to take drastic measures to keep her from hurting herself or the doctor. She had reached the point where she could be fairly stoical about such things and didn't kick or scream, although she still cried.

In spite of all this she would have gladly taken Karen's place had that been possible. We tried not to let her know when we were leaving for the clinic or lab with her little sister. Else we would find Cathy shut up in her room and physically sick by the time we returned.

She asked Karen one day, "It hurts, doesn't it?"

Karen said, "Not much." She was unusually sensitive to Cathy's concern for her, and that was the end of the conversation.

We were to live in the shadow of this odd blood pattern for years. It changed little and was always cause for speculation when we found ourselves under the care of a new doctor as we moved from place to place. It was much later, when she was almost eight, before the cause of the stomachaches were pinpointed. The high eosinophil count remained a mystery.

Those months remain a jumbled assortment of emotions. We have a clear-cut memory of some things, however. Our friends became brothers and sisters in those days. They were the uncles and aunts praying for a beloved little niece. They prayed for us and were there when we needed them; yet they did not become morbid nor allow us to do so.

We became aware, too, of our children's deep love for each other. There had never been any doubt of it, but their love had had no opportunity before to become selfless, each child thinking of the other and of the other's feelings.

Most precious of all was finding that God would not fail us, even in one of the hardest moments parents may be asked to bear—hearing a diagnosis that meant losing a child. I had tried to block the words out, but they were hammered into my heart. I didn't accept them nor find that I could bear them until I shared my burden with God. Then my grief was no less, but it was possible to live with it. Howard and I went through the days attending classes, going to meetings, trying not to turn completely inward. This was possible only because God was present with us and did not allow the grief to turn to despair. We were a long way from home, from physicians that had known Karen from birth, from those medical facilities that are so outstanding. Perhaps, had we been in the United States,

no doctor would have made such a prognosis. That is
something on which we could only conjecture.

As far away as we were from all these comforts, nearby was
the Comforter without whom all else would have been as
nought. I seldom failed to sleep well at night, because I knew
that things would work out according to God's purpose for our
lives. We did not know what would be his will for Karen; we
did know that it was his will for us to trust him regardless of
the outcome.

The change that took place in Karen during the next year
was almost unbelievable. She began growing and became
sturdy instead of fragile; not fat, but rounded out and solid
looking. She didn't become an extrovert overnight, but seeing
her blossom into a rambunctious child made it seem so by
comparison.

We rejoiced in her yelling and tearing around the house in
normal fashion. We realized everything was on an even keel
one day when she mischievously upset a house Cathy was
building and ran away saying, "You can't catch me, hah, hah!"
Cathy did catch her and, getting her down on the floor, tickled
her until she begged for help. Their roughhousing was music
to our ears.

Chapter 8

Having been born and reared in Georgia, we had a lot to learn about food, especially the Latin variety. I was the source of amusement to many of our friends who had lived most of their lives in Texas or California, and to whom such foods were as familiar as ham and grits were to us.

I just couldn't get tacos, enchiladas, tortillas, and tamales all straightened out in my thinking. Sue Lindwall, a tiny Californian and an excellent cook, patiently explained them to me more than once. Perhaps it was all mixed up with syntax, for I had to live a year in Mexico before I could order something from a menu and not be surprised at what I got.

I had never seen a tortilla, much less eaten one. So on the maid's day off one week we bought some, and I decided to fix tacos. According to instructions I had received, I knew they were supposed to be fried. I had failed to get the fact that they were to be fried first in a fold, then filled.

I took a limp, grey round and eyed it. It looked like a pancake left over from last month. But I courageously heaped it high with bits of meat, cheese and onions. I looked at the lettuce. Surely one didn't fry it, but how could it be poked in after frying?

As it turned out, I forgot all about the lettuce. The first

contrived combination I put into the frying pan unwound like a top and threw meat, cheese, and chopped onion all over the top of the stove. I fished all the bits, sizzling in the oil, out of the pan and sat down at the table to think over the problem.

It occurred to me, then, that I might be able to hold them together with toothpicks, like stuffed meat. I put three in the first one just to be sure. It held together until I dropped it into the pan, then the tortilla came apart. Everywhere I had stuck a toothpick it tore. "Some material!" I muttered. I picked up one of the tortillas still waiting to be stuffed and tried to take a bite. I almost tore out a tooth trying to disengage one small piece.

Howard and the children kept wandering through asking, "When's it going to be ready? Why don't you fix something else?" It was a temptation. But I hated to be bested in the battle, so I filled the tortillas, wrapped them, and got out some twine from the kitchen drawer. I tied granny knots in everyone of them after I had looped it around the rolled up mess. Then I laid them in another frying pan and poured hot oil over them from the first one.

The girls were delighted to get to untie their dinner, and one member of the family rashly observed that it was the best tortilla hash he had ever had. I still don't know why I created such a howl at school the next day when I described my ingenious methods.

The water supply in Costa Rica has been a serious problem for a long time because of being infested with intestinal parasites. I vaguely remembered studying about amoebas in biology, but now they became a household word as we admonished, "Don't drink the water out of the taps!"

"Why?"

"Because you'll get amoebas, that's why."

The only time it became a real nuisance not to drink water directly from the tap was when, brushing my teeth, I would find the water pitcher empty. By the time I had left a foamy trail down the stairs to get a refill, I was tempted to take a chance the next time. Everytime I weakened, one of our friends would discover that he had amoebas of one or more classes and would have to start on medication to get rid of them. A look at their pea-green faces would convince me that it was worth trying a little longer. The medicine poisons the amoebas and often is a mild poison to the host. Reactions ranged from a mild sense of nausea to the violent I-wish-I-could-die refrain.

For the most part, we had little to worry about in foods. We didn't eat salads and uncooked vegetables in out-of-the-way places. Most of our food was cooked for such long periods of time that it was quite safe. One thing that Blanca liked to fix was *olla de carne* which means "kettle of meat." The dish consisted of a large bone with a little meat clinging to it and cooked in its own clear broth with whole vegetables such as *chayotes, ayotes,* potatoes, carrots, and sometimes sweet potatoes.

After the first visit to the meat market, I gladly relinquished the job of meat-buying to Blanca or Howard. Most of the meat was beef, unaged and usually butchered the morning of the day it was to be sold. I stood and watched them unload great hunks of meat off a cart. A boy heaved a piece over his head and back and, bent almost double, staggered into the small shop with it. By the time he had transferred a few hunks, his hair was the color of henna, and blood was caked in rivulets down his back and chest. An old mongrel dog followed every step he made, licking the meat as he tagged along behind.

The boy threw the meat down on the counter, and the

butcher put it on hooks to hang from the ceiling. There the slabs of meat rotated gently in the breeze and took on a mottled appearance as swarms of flies settled in to cover it. Right then I mentally vowed to become a vegetarian.

Later when I saw that the meat had to be cooked in a pressure cooker at least a couple of hours to make it chewable, I decided it was safe. There was a lot to be desired in the flavor after cooking so long, but this was camouflaged by sauces, usually of tomatoes and onions.

Every Tuesday morning at four-thirty, Blanca went to the market downtown to buy fruits and vegetables for the week. She and her sister Marina went together on the bus. Later, loaded with produce that was brought in fresh that morning from outlying farms, they took a taxi home. All of the vegetables and fruits were washed thoroughly. Those not to be cooked were soaked in an iodine solution for about a half hour, then boiling water was poured over them. This turned the bananas black although it didn't affect the taste. For a long time after we returned to the States, Karen eyed yellow bananas with suspicion.

We had field-ripened fresh pineapple, oranges, bananas, mangoes, and many other fruits unknown to us until that time. Apples were scarce and very expensive. We saw peaches one time during the year but passed them by. One peach cost fifty cents.

My taste buds were homesick for things like turnip greens, okra, tender corn, spring lettuce, and the like. But, being human, when I returned to Georgia I fussed about the unsweet pineapple and small bananas.

One of the things we came to appreciate and missed later was the leisurely dinner served in many courses. Food is appreciated in Latin America, and there is an old-world approach to the preparation and serving of it in the hotels and larger restaurants. A first course of fruit is followed by soup; the soup by a fish course; then salad and the main course. After dessert comes a demitasse, and the whole thing can easily consume two hours.

We were fortunate to have pasteurized milk in San José. This is yet to be seen in many Central and South American countries. There was one place where we could even get banana splits and sundaes. It involved a bus ride and hike of several blocks since we didn't have a car, but the girls were always ready to go whenever someone mentioned ice cream. When we went the first time, we were with another person and didn't pay any attention to the route we took. Cathy was overjoyed to see a miniature golf course nearby.

"Can we come back and play?" She jumped up and down. "Oh, please, can we come back?"

We promised. On our first free day we took off in the general direction we remembered, got off the bus, and started walking. After nineteen or twenty blocks with no ice cream parlor sighted nor anything that looked like a miniature golf course, we angled off to the right. Nothing looked familiar.

By that time we had been walking for over an hour, and Karen was griping with every step she took. Her complaining soon changed to "Take me, Daddy," and daddy was soon complaining as he jogged along carrying her on his back. We were in the middle of a residential section when a taxi came cruising down the street. Howard put Karen down and almost walked in front of the car to stop it.

We got in wearily and sat back. The driver asked us where we wanted to go. We had been in Costa Rica only a couple of weeks, and this was our first trip out by ourselves. Howard said to me, "I'm not going to be licked by this thing!"

He said to the driver in halting Spanish, "We want to go . . ." and stopped. He turned to me. "How in the world do you say 'miniature golf-course?' "

I looked pained. "Dear, I don't even know how to say golf."

He looked at Cathy. She was picking up the language faster than we were, but she just shrugged, "I don't know."

The driver had pulled over to the curb by this time and was leaning over the back of the seat following our exchange of words without understanding any of it. After several minutes he said, freely translated, "Okay, Mac, where to"?

Howard sighed. "I could tell him to take us home. I've got the address memorized." It was necessary to memorize addresses because street names and numbers weren't used. Our address was: *La entrada principal de La Granja, la casa de dos pisos de color azul.* This said we lived at the main entrance to the chicken farm (long since closed down) in the two-story blue house.

Cathy and Karen put up a united howl. The driver slumped down in his seat and whimpered.

Howard opened the door, got out of the car, and stood on the sidewalk. The man looked up to see what he was doing, and my undaunted husband bent over in a pantomine of holding a golf club and teed off. The driver didn't say a word. He slid over to that side of the car and rested his chin on the window, gazing at Howard in fascination. Howard swung again, following through nicely.

By this time we had attracted a crowd. Someone asked the driver what was going on. He made some comment about crazy North Americans, and that seemed to satisfy everyone. He threw up his hands and told Howard to get in and he'd take us where he thought we wanted to go.

When we got downtown I was sure he didn't have a

glimmer of an idea of what we wanted, but he had put up with us so long that we were afraid to say anything. After weaving in and out of traffic and up and down narrow streets through a part of town unknown to us, he pulled up in front of a store on the corner and got out to open the door.

We both laughed to keep from crying when we saw that the store window was full of walking sticks and canes. The pantomine of a bent over man had gotten through to our driver.

Howard said, "Well, I didn't think I looked that bad!" Then he shook his head. "I hate to disillusion him."

The man was waiting for us to get out, and I'm sure he was ready to wish us a hearty good-bye. We sat still, and he stuck in a puzzled, good-natured face to ask us, "What's the matter? Didn't I bring you where you wanted to go?"

Four heads shook in unison. We couldn't apologize or commiserate with him for having such bad luck. The truth was he was stuck with us until he got us to the miniature golf course or home.

Howard got out and tried again. He said, "I don't want a stick. I want to play." The girls snickered over that one. "Daddy wants to play." He said, "Be quiet! No, not you," he said to the driver, forgetting he was using English. Then in Spanish he said, "It's a game. You use a stick. A game . . . you know."

The light seemed to have dawned for the driver because he got back in and we took off, this time for the opposite side of town. Since we hadn't gone through town to get there before, we were afraid he was wrong but decided not to say anything since there might be two. We rode for several minutes through a lovely suburb. When we pulled up in front of a building Howard said, "Oh no! It's the country club.

The man's beaming face fell flat when he looked around at us. He was so sure this time, and there we were sitting so dejectedly. "But, señor, this is where they play with the little stick, no?"

Howard said, "Sí, sí."

"Why don't you get out then?" He was brightening up again.

I shook my head. Howard shook his head. The children were almost past moving. Daddy tried again. "It's for the children. Not for us."

"Oh! *Golfito!* Why didn't you say so?" With that he wheeled down the drive and had us through town in no time at all.

Golfito. In time we were to learn that many times a Spanish ending to an English word was the formula. *Golfito* —little golf.

We arrived at the miniature golf course and I said, "All out, girls."

Karen started crying. "I want an ice cream cone."

Cathy chimed in. "I do, too."

Howard brushed his hand over his hair. "You mean you don't want to play miniature golf?"

Both of them were tired and hungry. The sun had almost gone down, and the course looked damp and unappealing.

Poor daddy looked at the driver and declared, "He'll never believe this."

I looked at the man. He had his hat pulled down over his ears and was hunched over the steering wheel as if to ward off a blow from the rear. "I know," he said. "Where to?"

We ended up at the ice cream parlor hoping the large tip would give the man a new lease on life. I felt reckless and ordered something that sounded exotic. It turned out to be a banana split without a banana.

Food was only one of the many new experiences that enchanted us with Costa Rica. We became less provincial in thoughts and attitudes, discovering again and again that there was seldom only one right way of doing things. The alternates might not be better, but many times they were just as good and certainly different.

Different was an overused word for us, but a handy one. We could always say, "Well, it's different," until we could make up our minds about it. We, ourselves, were so different from those around us, not just by dint of our background, but by our beliefs. It isn't always easy to be different, to be set apart. The children felt it more than we did as children fear nonconformity. But even they realized that in our case the difference was that God was a reality in our lives.

Chapter 9

During the first term of our year in Costa Rica, twenty Southern Baptist families were living there, including two resident missionary families, the Tom Hills and the Laverne Gregorys. In San José and the neighboring towns that we could reach by bus without taking all day were some eight or ten churches and missions. We tried to spread out so that one church wouldn't be swamped with missionaries but still leave every one enough choice so that he would be happy in his church work.

For a while it was like musical chairs. Each family visited some of the churches, if not all of them, before making a decision. We decided to join the church in Heredia, a small city close to San José. We attended alone until Guy and Judy Williamson joined during our last term.

To get to the church we walked to a corner where we caught a bus for town. Then we walked over a few blocks to get on the small bus going to Heredia. It wound up and down hills, over long bridges, and through lovely *fincas,* for about thirty minutes. The time depended on when the bus left and how many stops it had to make, so we tried to allow about two hours for the journey from house to church. From the bus stop in Heredia to the church was a walk of several blocks through town, across the plaza past the water fountains, and down a narrow street.

Sometimes we arrived early and stopped for a Coke at a small pastry shop. Other times we had to run through town to arrive in time for Sunday School. The first Sunday we attended the church in Heredia, Laverne Gregory took us. He was on his way to preach in another church, but he took enough time to go in with us and introduce us to the pastor. Then he left, and we were on our own.

Don Oscar was an imposing figure, although slender in build. He looked like a Spanish don of olden days with his neatly groomed mustache, and he was the epitome of charm and politeness. He said something to me just as Laverne's car drove off, and I looked around for someone to help me. Howard just shrugged his shoulders which meant, "Your guess is as good as mine."

Don Oscar repeated his request, and at least I knew that it was a request because of the inflection. Finally he took me by the arm, led me to the piano, and seated me with an out-flung arm and a bow from the waist. He pointed to the number and raised his eyebrows. I was so relieved to know what he wanted that I nodded even though I didn't recognize the hymn.

He took his place at the rostrum, said a few words, and picked up his hymn book. Then he nodded in my direction, and I nervously played the opening bars. I almost jumped off the bench when a violin sounded in my ear, picking up the music on the second bar. I looked over my left shoulder and saw an elderly man sawing at the strings, the tip of his bow grazing my hair. We got through that song without my head being punctured, but I kept trying to edge down the bench. Every time I moved, he moved a little, too.

After the hymn, Don Oscar read from the Bible. Every one stood to read. Then he picked up his hymn book again and said something. I thought, Oh my goodness! Is he going to have to come down off the platform and point it out to me?

But the violinist leaned over and turned the page for me, pointing to the song. I almost kissed him. It was difficult to play along with him, as he had his own timing for each hymn; but, then, the congregation sang along at another pace, and the pastor boomed out over them all at still a different tempo. So it hardly mattered. He was my friend for life after that morning.

By virtue of being the only pianist in the congregation, I played for all the services. After awhile the pastor was kind enough to write out the order of service with the numbers of the hymns. This made it less painful for me, but I still could not relax as he had a habit of handing me a book or a sheet of music on his way to the platform and announcing that he would sing a special right before he sang it.

There was one other thing that threatened to give me nervous hives. On many occasions a four- or five-piece ensemble would visit to play for the services, and I was supposed to accompany the saxophone, clarinet, trumpet, accordian, and drums for anything the group wanted to play. This orchestra was composed of members of a family who had played for dances before their conversion, and they had a swing-and-sway style much like Sammy Kaye. The congregation couldn't keep its feet still while singing even the most sedate hymns. My own left foot began patting a jazz beat before I realized it. The ensemble had a catching syncopation to "There's Power in the Blood," and the people loved it. I thought: Shades of Handel! but I bounced along too.

We had not realized how closely our attendance was

checked until we received a telegram one Monday from the pastor. Due to illness we had been absent two Sundays. The telegram was rather strongly worded, "Your continued absence is deplored. You will be in your place on Sunday." We wondered how the average church member in the States would react to such a summons. Would attendance improve or would the churches close?

Howard often went out to the church during the week to help the men with some of the interior construction that had not been finished. He enjoyed working alongside them and getting to know them better. At the end of the year when we were leaving, the church had a farewell service and presented us with a lovely lace tablecloth. It was banquet size and represented so much money we were loath to take it.

One of the men Howard had worked with slipped up and told him, "Go on and take it. We sometimes give wooden plaques, but some of us men talked the pastor into getting you something you can use." He laughed. "Well, something your wife can use anyway."

From time to time during that year, we became most discouraged with our slow pace of learning and lack of ability to communicate the message that had brought us to Costa Rica in the first place. Then we would learn something about a fellow church member that made us ashamed of our little faith. Almost every one had an inspiring story of trust in the Lord. We talked to men who had lost good jobs because they were evangelicals. Others had faced physical persecution because of their beliefs. None of them found it easy to live and work in the tightly knit Catholic community.

We experienced a little of this difficulty during the week of revival held in the spring. Paint was thrown over the front of our church, and words were painted on the sidewalk—derogatory remarks that had to be walked over in order to enter.

During the services rocks were often thrown at the tin roof. The first time this happened I jumped as if the rock had made contact with me. Immediately, I was embarrassed. The preacher did not twitch a muscle; the others sat as still as if there had not been the slightest sound.

On Sunday, the last day of the revival, a band marched down the street playing at top volume. The church is on a little traveled street that is not on the regular route for parades. But on it came. It marked cadence in front of the church for several moments and then turned down the side street. The noise was deafening. The evangelist had to stop in the middle of his message. As the noise faded into the distance, he picked up his thought and continued. The marchers turned, and the music grew in volume as the band approached the church again. The man waited in silence, his head bowed. At last the band marched out of hearing, and he finished his sermon.

There were twenty men, women, and young people who made professions of faith that morning. The vestibule was filled with curious onlookers who had followed the parade, then were drawn inside to see what was going on. The pastor moved quickly and gave out dozens of tracts and marked copies of the New Testament. We were to see several of these people become regular attendants in church before we left.

Howard visited the small town of Naranjo one Sunday with Laverne Gregory. During the service a young girl named Alicia got up to say something. Her pastor rose, put his hand on her shoulder and said, "Before Alicia says anything, I want to tell you something. As most of you know, she graduated from elementary school last week. That night the auditorium was filled with people. Several of you were there. After the songs and speeches came the time for the awards. All of the children were excited over the award to be given to the best student. Many of them had worked hard for it. The director got up and made a lengthy explanation of one special award. Among other things he said, 'This award is given for two reasons: to honor the diligent efforts of the student and to encourage him to continue his good work.' Everyone waited with bated breath as he picked up the scroll to read the name. He hesitated and then said, 'This award was to be given to Alicia G. There is no doubt that she is the best student. But receiving this award should indicate the overall excellence of the student. Alicia fails in one respect—she is not a member of the recognized Church. Therefore we present the award to Alfredo M.' "

The pastor then put his arm around the child's shoulders and added, "Now she would like to give her testimony."

Howard leaned forward to catch her words. He wondered what the girl could say after being publicly humiliated and denied an award rightfully hers.

Alicia's words were strong and clear. "I love Jesus. When I grow up I want to study to be a missionary. Then I will come back here and teach. I want all these people to learn to love Jesus too."

Chapter 10

We usually studied until late at night and fell into bed exhausted. One night I was shaken from a deep sleep. I thought my husband was shaking me awake and I sat up in bed irritated.

"If you want to tell me something, tell me!" I grumbled. "But stop pushing!"

He did not reply.

Then I saw him. He was standing at the foot of the bed, hanging on to the bedpost and rocking with laughter. A bit miffed at this joke-playing in the middle of the night, I yanked the blankets up to my chin and went back to sleep.

The next morning I found out that Howard had not rattled me out of my sleep by shaking the bedpost. An earthquake had come in the night, a fairly heavy tremor, rattling quite a few people from their dreams. Howard had been hanging on to the bedpost to maintain his balance.

We were to live through several such tremors during our year in San José. Three deserve mention. The first one made me mad at being awakened, the second one amused me, and the third one almost scared me to death.

The second one occurred during refreshment period one morning at school. A friend and I had decided to use the time to study for our next class in grammar. Sitting in one of the small classrooms off the main hall, we suddenly became aware of the peculiar sensation of the floor undulating beneath us. When the windows began going in and out at impossible angles, we eased out of our chairs and started toward the door. We had been told to stand inside a door frame during a quake as this was the safest spot to be found inside a building.

It almost proved to be our undoing. We reached the door, only to be mobbed by a group of frantic teachers pushing and shoving, thinking only of getting into the room. We got jolted to the side by shoulders, elbows, and hands.

This, instead of scaring us, was funny. Perhaps the sight of so much uncontrolled fear, when we could see no real cause for panic, gave us a case of nervous giggles. Later, we had only to recall the two of us facing that wave of hysterical humanity to break out in gales of laughter. We came to the more sober conclusion, after the third tremor, that perhaps our good humor stemmed from being abysmally ignorant rather than brave. Those people, having lived all their lives in Costa Rica, knew the destruction that was possible, and their actions revealed this awareness.

There are no adequate words with which to describe an earthquake. It goes beyond the boundary of language and enters the realm of raw emotions. Sea sickness or air sickness can cause a person to say with meaning, "Just let me get my feet on good old mother earth, and I'll never sail or fly again for the rest of my life."

Mother earth has long been the symbol of stability and security. When this symbol is shattered, it leaves no other in its place. There is no visible place of safety.

One evening, in the spring, my husband and Bill Gray were sitting at the table in the dining room studying together.

I was in bed reading, and the children were in their room asleep.

We had no warning. The earthquake began full-blown. I jumped out of bed to get to the children. A long wail reached my ears, quickly rising to the crescendo of a shriek and hanging there without changing tone. A little pajama-clad form came plummeting through the hall and crashed into me headfirst. Karen had been thrown from her bed and she landed on the floor, almost running. Cathy followed on her heels, speechless with fright.

I attempted to put on my robe, hold Karen, and calm Cathy, all the time trying to get us headed toward the stairs. The great panels of glass were bending and swaying. The walls went in and out, up and down. The floor was in constant motion. We found it hard to stay on our feet.

Howard's head appeared in the stair well, but he seemed to be standing still. It was no mere impression. As he put one foot down and picked up the other one to place it on the next step, the stairs shifted back and forth, and he was walking in one place as on a treadmill. He finally discovered that he could move upward only if he took two steps at a time. In a second, then, he was with us, comforting the children and deciding the best thing to do.

The tremor stopped, and we made our way down the long flight of stairs. Then it began again, and the lights went out. We got out the front door and onto the sidewalk and looked back. The house was swaying out over us and then snapping back into place. It swayed, buckled, and snapped. I mentally thanked the builder for all the looseness in the house, the wide spaces between the sliding doors and windows that had caused me so much grief in my never-ending battle with the flies and mosquitoes.

Howard cupped his hands over his mouth and yelled, "Bill, are you all all right?" Bill had run out the front door to their apartment when the shake started, and now the house was dark and silent.

Howard had just started to holler again when the front door was yanked open and Bill bellowed, "What are you doing standing out there? Get in out from under those wires!"

We made it up the front steps and found Pinky, his wife, and the children, Brad and Anna Harriet, coming down the steps from upstairs. There was some comfort in numbers.

Then we began to hear the cries of people all around us as they fled into the streets calling loudly to their patron saints. This unearthly caterwaul heightened the sense of being in the middle of a nightmare.

The third tremor began. Cathy had gone over and picked up Anna Harriet; she dropped her and ran over to huddle next to Karen and me on the steps. Anna Harriet, a little blonde two-year old, bounced up and down on the couch delighted with the shaking she was getting.

We could hardly believe it when we were told later that each tremor had lasted only nineteen or twenty seconds. Our feelings were salved when we found that it had been the most severe quake recorded in almost fifty years in that country. The one fifty years before had completely destroyed the nearby city of Cartago.

Mild tremors occurred off and on all night, but we awakened to a beautiful, cloudless day. The morning at school was spent in hearing all the tales our friends and teachers had to relate. One family rushed out into the street and was told by a neighbor that the safest place for them would be under their dining table. They hurried back in, crawled under the table, and spent the night huddled on the hard tile floor.

Another family with a small baby also rushed out looking for a safer place. Father suddenly recalled that he was responsible for their United States passports. Going back into the house, he remembered they had no food for the baby. He grabbed passports and jars of baby food, crammed them into a large *bolsa,* and started out the door. Then he turned back. He had been heating coffee when the shake started, so he jammed pot and all into the bag and ran out again in search of his family.

In the days following the shakeup we found that almost every individual had a story to relate concerning that night. Fortunately, only a few buildings were seriously damaged and no one was killed, although there were several deaths from heart attacks.

One of our friends, even though feeling compassion for her maid, found a funny side to her fears in the night. The maid started praying aloud to her patron saint, but as the shakes became harder and she was rocked from her knees, she bypassed all the saints and began directing her prayers to God, perhaps for the first time in her life.

It was Blanca's night out and she was on her way home from town. Since it was late she took a taxi. They had stopped for a traffic light when the first tremor began. Almost all the taxis were small, foreign-made cars, and this little bug was bounced up and placed neatly on the sidewalk. The curb was so high the driver couldn't get the car off, so he locked it and walked away in disgust.

Blanca was left several blocks from home and was forced to walk the rest of the way. She came stomping in so furious at the cab driver that she seemed totally unaware of the real dangers she had faced.

When the third tremor had died down that night and

another one didn't start immediately, Bill and Howard decided to check on the Williamsons, who lived around the corner from us. They had been in Costa Rica only a few days, and we thought they might be more alarmed than we were, not having had the initiation of lighter earthquakes.

Judy met them at the door. "I'm going home." Guy was laughing by that time, and the children hadn't even waked up. Judy finally joined in the laughter saying, "Well, I guess I won't go right now. But I can do without any more welcomes like this."

So we were, in turn, irritated, amused, and frightened by these terrible manifestations of nature's power. We were made aware again of how inadequate we are, how powerless we can become. The words, "On Christ, the solid rock, I stand, all other ground is sinking sand," became reality for us that night. Although we were terrified, we had an inner security that was not affected by outward circumstances.

The crucified Christ hanging on the crosses in the cathedrals and churches offered little comfort to the panic-stricken people during those dark hours. How we longed to share with them our living God, unchanging, eternal, the Rock of Ages.

Chapter 11

We were in the doldrums. Study had lost its newness. With several months still before us, we found ourselves wishing for a change of scenery for a day or so. Several of our friends had been to Puntarenas on the Pacific Ocean and recommended it as a wonderful place to go. Dave and Bettye Stull shared our desire to get away, so we made our plans and set out for two days of sun and water.

We went by train, a long slow ride through the mountains down to the coast. The scenery changed by the hour as we wound through forest and plain, mountain and valley. At each stop the food venders hopped on board with fruit, hot dishes of chicken, eggs, tacos, and rice. We bought some roasted cashews and tried the fruit of the cashew plant. It is about the size of a large peach and with much the same coloration. The nut forms a handle for the fruit which tasted to me like a wild cross between a cantaloupe and a persimmon.

The leisurely trip suited our needs exactly. We even enjoyed the unexplained stops made in the middle of fields and rocky mountain passes.

After riding for three hours we began to look for the ocean, and as the train came to a grinding stop high in the mountains we caught a glimpse of it through the trees. Howard unpacked his camera and leaned out of the window to take a picture. Dissatisfied with the perspective he jumped off the train to take one from the edge of the cliff and had been gone only a moment when the train started to move.

It gained momentum rapidly as it went down the mountain incline. Dave, Bettye, and I were hanging out the window yelling to Howard to run and catch the steps at the end of the observation car. He started sprinting down the side of the tracks, laughing and waving to us as he ran. Suddenly he disappeared. He had fallen headlong into a hole, and for a moment all we could see was a great cloud of dust rising from the spot.

We lost all hope of his catching the train and began to look for someone who could stop it. There wasn't a button to push nor a cord to pull, and the conductor wasn't in sight. The only word I could think to yell was *esquina* which means "corner" and was used on the busses in the city when the cord couldn't be reached to signal a stop. It just didn't seem to be a proper word to use in the middle of the mountains.

Dave rushed off to find someone, somewhere, and Bettye and I went back to the observation car to see if we could see any of the remains. It was quite a surprise to see Howard sprinting along the edge of the tracks again, making such good time in spite of a limping run that he swung upon the steps at the back just as the train came to another of its abrupt halts. Dave hadn't found anyone; it was just time to stop again.

We sadly surveyed the damage. Howard was covered in a thick, unyielding layer of dust; he was battered and scratched from top to bottom. As he undressed later, he found a mysterious circle imprinted on his chest. It was red, round, and obviously made from striking an object with force. After some thought he got out his camera and looked. The lens fit the impression exactly; it wasn't broken, but his chest was branded.

When the train pulled into Puntarenas, the children were impatient to get to the beach. So, as soon as we checked into the motel, they ran out to the sand. We followed, and everyone stopped in astonishment. The whole setting could have been taken from the South Pacific. The rugged mountains came down almost to the shore, and the broad stretch of beach was fringed with palms dipping toward the water. The waves rode high and left fingers of froth on the sand. But all this beauty was wasted on the children at that moment for they were staring at the sand in which we were standing. It was black; not dirty sand, but a pearly black that glistened in the sun. They picked it up, let it sift through their fingers, and then convinced that it was really sand, went whooping along the water.

I can get sunburned hanging out the clothes, so I spread suntan lotion generously over myself and the children. Howard is darker than I and tans easily, but he used the lotion on his back as he stretched out on a towel. After lying there about thirty minutes, he decided to go back to the room and treat some of the scratches and bruises. The children played happily for more than an hour, then we went back in for a rest before dinner.

I found my husband in the deepest of miseries. Not only did he ache from his fall, but for the first time in his life he was blistered. He said, "Deliver me from black sand. I must be allergic to it." He couldn't lie on his stomach because of the bruises, and he couldn't rest on his back because he was lobster red on his shoulders and the back of his legs.

In spite of this we had a good two days there. Howard had to move around slowly, but the children swam and played and we were able to rest and unwind. The last night we decided to have a weiner roast on the beach and watch the moon come up. It was a beautiful sight with the waves pounding the beach and breaking their white crests into spray that filled the air.

We ate, then sat and talked, leaning against some of the huge logs that were scattered along the shore. Little Dave and Cathy built forts and castles in the sand. Debbie and Karen made a collection of shells. We were reluctant to go in, but we had to be up early the next day to catch the train. A last lingering look etched on our memories the beauty of this place.

As we gathered up towels and the remains of the picnic Howard said, "You know, I haven't been swimming at all. I believe I'll go back and put on my trunks and take a plunge. At least I won't get sunburned now."

He was heading toward the beach as we started back to the motel, so we didn't see the fiasco that followed. He hit the surf running and made a clean dive into one of the towering breakers. Just as he made contact with the water the draw string on his trunks snapped and they fell to his ankles. He found himself in deep water, pummeled by the crashing waves and trying to extract himself from his bathing suit before he drowned. He was kicking and pulling while being tossed about as easily as a small log.

With one mighty kick he got his right foot free and was able to twist around to pull off his trunks. He headed back for the beach and his only comment after he told me about it was, "It's a wonder it wasn't broad daylight on a crowded beach!"

He was glad to get on the train the next morning, and the wanderlust didn't strike him nearly so hard again for months. He was morose over the fact that I couldn't look at him without dissolving into what he called "braying like a burro."

The trip was more than I could think about without laughing, and I became persona non grata with him.

I was truly sorry for all the pain he was suffering and would have undone the series of events could I have managed. But all my compassion couldn't erase the pictures of that weekend that would come leaping into my mind. So when I awoke at night and thought about it, I put my head under the pillow to keep from waking him with my "braying."

Chapter *12*

One afternoon I was sprawled across the bed reading when Howard walked in and tossed an envelope to me. I took out the card, read it, and stuck it in my book. I didn't realize he was still standing there until he spoke. "You'd better look at that a little more carefully. We're to be in it."

"It" I discovered on second glance was a wedding. The invitation was beautifully engraved on a double card. Later on I made a translation of the invitation to send home to our families. Since I knew the names of the Costa Rican couple would mean nothing to them, I used our names. On the left-hand side, with the substitutions, it read:

Taylor Young Evans
and
Cora Stephens of Young
have the pleasure of inviting you and your family
to the marriage of their daughter
NORMA
to Mr.
HOWARD STEVENS CULPEPPER

On the right-hand side:

Homer Stevens Harmon
and
Marilizzie Culpepper of Stevens
have the pleasure of inviting you and your family
to the marriage of their son
HOWARD
to Miss
NORMA YOUNG STEPHENS

Across the bottom of the invitation was the date and place along with an additional invitation to the reception afterwards.

The maiden name of the mother is a part of the surname, although many times the person will add only the initial of his mother's name. Howard is Howard Stevens Culpepper but he may sign his name as Howard Stevens C. Many times the person is called by both names such as Mr. Stevens Culpepper.

The names on the cards I held in my hand that day were slightly familiar, but I wasn't sure. "Do I know them?" I asked.

Howard said, "He works in the associational office, and I think we've met her, but I don't remember when."

My next question was, "Did you say we were going to be *in* the wedding?"

"That's right."

Sometimes my husband delights in making me pull out all the details, point by point, but this time I didn't play.

He grinned and I glared at him. He cleared his throat. "We're going to be *padrinos*."

"We're going to be what?" I asked.

"*Padrinos*."

"I heard what you said. What does it mean?" I queried testily.

He pulled his nose, a characteristic gesture when he is at a loss for words or is thinking. "I was afraid you'd ask that. I don't know what it is but I accepted for us."

I said, "Oh, joy!" and started looking in the dictionary. It didn't help much. There were several definitions such as godfather; second, in a duel (I discarded that one); best man; patron, protector.

"Best man" was the only word that seemed to relate to a wedding. "Did you say we're to serve? Both of us?"

Howard nodded. "I don't suppose it means best man then. Well, don't worry about it. I guess someone will tell us what it's all about."

The next day we discovered that several of our friends had been asked to serve as *padrinos* too. Tom and Cornice Hill took pity on us and explained that we were to be witnesses and would stand in the wedding party. Implicit in this honor was the obligation to give a gift.

This wasn't so simple. The gifts were to be something beautiful and nonutilitarian. We couldn't think of things like pots and pans. One nice saleslady almost swooned when we asked her if towels would serve as our gift. She delivered a long lecture on the duty of *padrinos* to provide the elegant, luxurious things for the new home. We finally compromised on a set of glass bowls.

When the day arrived for the wedding, we were more nervous than the bride and groom. We were told to be at the church early, so we arrived at five o'clock since the wedding was to be at six. People were milling around, and no one seemed to be in charge.

One of the student missionaries, Barbara Hintze, had been asked to play. It was her first experience, too, to participate in a Costa Rican wedding. She began playing soft music at five-thirty. At six o'clock we still hadn't seen anyone that looked like a bride or groom. At six thirty-five some of the bridesmaids came in a rush down the sidewalk and giggled their way into the room off the left of the vestibule.

By this time Barbara was stopping occasionally to rub some feeling back into her fingers. I kept wiggling my toes trying to keep my feet from going to sleep. I don't know why we remained standing. We could have sat down in the auditorium, but felt almost as though we were on call for a stage production and so stayed in our places.

When the hands of the clock began to creep close to seven, Howard whispered, "I think they eloped. You ready to go?"

I was ready. But just then the groom arrived with his parents. They entered the room on the right, and all was quiet again except for the bustling in and out of the bridesmaids. They seemed to be in various stages of dress. When the door swung open, we caught a glimpse of hair being teased, sashes being stitched, and one girl taking off her makeup, evidently prior to putting on fresh.

It looked like a long winter's wait, but then a lady came to organize the *padrinos,* and we soon saw that all the people we thought were guests were to be witnesses too. Altogether there were twenty-six of us. Later as we stood around the altar and I could see the people, it seemed to me we had more up front than were in the pews.

To my relief we were placed near the end of the line. This meant that we could follow those in front of us and hope they knew what to do. The man and woman behind us were well dressed in quiet, good taste. He looked like a banker in his dark suit, and she was dressed in a royal blue suit of mohair that could have come from Paris. I relaxed. Surely they knew the rules of the game.

We stood at attention in the line for several minutes. Nothing happened. The line got ragged as everyone began to talk and shift around. Barbara cast despairing glances toward the rear but kept on playing.

At seven-thirty the bride came rushing in, leaving her parents to get out of the taxi, and scattered everyone as she dashed into the room with her attendants. We straightened the line again and waited. Again nothing happened. I had gotten over my stage fright pretty well by that time, but Howard told me I was numb, not courageous.

At seven forty-five the lady rearranged us, opened the doors to the rooms on the right and left, and nodded in the general direction of the organ. Barbara, with evident relief, began Mendelssohn's "Wedding March."

The bridesmaids and groomsmen began their slow march down the aisle. The girls were dressed in bouffant, waltz-length gowns; two were in blue, two in turquoise, and two in yellow. The men wore dark blue suits.

Then, although I saw no signal, we were on our way to the altar. On the way down we comported ourselves well, I think. That is, we followed those in front of us and didn't step on their heels, nor go so slowly that we blocked the couple behind us. We got to the front right behind our dignified friends. When everyone stopped we were all in a tight little bunch. Someone made a fanning-out motion, and the human Gordian knot moved an inch or two. Our lady director came up behind us whispering directions in everyone's ear. "Move back and out. Move back and out." Apparently we were all new at the job, but she finally got a path cleared for the bride and groom.

By this time the organist had played the wedding march through about three times. When all twenty-six of us were still and more or less in place, she struck the opening cord again with more emphasis, and the little flower girl made a skipping start down the aisle. She looked around and, seeing so many people, she ducked her head and put one foot in front of the other so slowly that we despaired of her ever reaching the front. When she did get to the steps of the platform, she wheeled around on one foot to see who was coming behind her and forgot to go up and stand with the bridesmaids.

The groom then paced slowly down the aisle with his mother on his arm, and behind them came the bride clinging to the arm of her father. She was lovely. Her wedding dress looked like an original. It was of white lace with tiny buttons all the way down the front and fitted her to perfection. Had I been wont to put a price on such a dress in the States, I would have said several hundred dollars, but I had been window shopping too many times in San José to believe that this stunning creation cost more than twenty-five dollars. On closer examination of most wedding dresses the reason was obvious. The material was usually of the cheapest, but the manner in which they were made covered up the imperfections of the cloth. I remarked one day to a friend that I couldn't understand how they could bear to put so much workmanship into something that wouldn't last past one wearing. She amusedly pointed out that only one wearing was required.

When the bride and her father reached the altar, he and the groom's mother stepped back, and the young man and woman stood side by side. Part of the ceremony was familiar, but the sermon in the middle was an innovation for us. It was short enough, about ten minutes of exhortation for a Christian home. But now my feet were past the numb stage, and I kept putting my weight first on one, then the other, trying to keep from yelling out loud.

Howard leaned over and whispered in my ear, "What kind of strange dance are you doing?"

I stopped shifting, and he pulled me back against him to rest, knowing full well why I was so fidgety. Then it was over, and the newlyweds made a dash down the aisle. I made a dash for the nearest pew and tried to decide if I dared take my shoes off, could I ever hope to get them on again?

I didn't have time to decide because someone said, "Come on. You can't goof off now. We've got to go to the reception."

I drooped. But when we walked into the large social hall in the annex of the church, my spirits picked up. Long tables placed in U form and covered with white paper filled the room. There were chairs for everyone. Even though many had come from the children's Sunday School rooms, they were welcome. We sat down and were passed napkins filled with small sandwiches and cookies.

If possible, I was hungrier than I was tired. I bit into my sandwich and had half-eaten it when Howard nudged me and said wickedly, "I thought you didn't like cold re-fried beans."

I gulped and peeked at the filling of my sandwich. "It tastes like ambrosia," I lied. I ate it all and then the cookies. I noticed some of our friends unobtrusively wrapping their sandwiches in napkins, but they must have had an early supper.

By this time the bride was busily cutting an enormous cake, and we were served small pieces. I was thinking longingly of home, the refrigerator, and bed—in that order. But when we started out the door, one of our more knowledgeable friends stopped us. "Where do you think you're going? You know you can't leave before the bride and groom do."

We knew we shouldn't, but it was so late we had decided

they weren't going to leave. Properly chastened, we sat down in two small chairs near the door until at last—about an hour later—they began making their farewells. It was then we learned that they had been waiting until train time to go to the station and leave on their honeymoon.

As they left, the radiance of their faces cleared away our tiredness. We thought of how two lives dedicated to God's work in Costa Rica could work miracles in the years to come. Criticism, revilement, and discrimination would no doubt be present throughout their lives as they would live among those who could not or would not understand them. That they could be so happy, embarking on a difficult life because they loved God, put a new song in our hearts and made the long walk to the bus corner less tedious.

Chapter 13

"Come on. Stop that studying and let's go to town." Howard pulled me up out of the chair and headed me toward the door.

"If you'll just wait a minute, I'll gladly go. But let me put on my shoes."

It was raining, as it usually did in the afternoon, so I put on rain boots and rain coat and gathered up the umbrellas. Howard was convinced that he gained more use of Spanish by getting out and talking to people than I did by studying. So occasionally, he made me leave my books and go with him.

I enjoyed going. I liked to window shop and find the little stores tucked back in the side streets. Every store was a speciality house. To get material for a dress I went to one shop. I had to find another one for the pattern and still a third for thread, buttons, and pins.

As we sloshed along in the rain I asked, "Do we have some special place to go, or are we just going nowhere in particular?"

He smiled. "Mr. Ali told me to come in this afternoon. He has something he wants to show us."

Mr. Ali owned a gift shop with many items from his native country, India. We had spent hours looking at the ivory carvings, brass bells, woven rugs, and wooden chests, as well as things from Panama and Guatemala. I had bought a tablecloth from Hong Kong that had come by way of Panama and skirts for myself and the children from Guatemala. Howard visited with him for a few minutes almost every afternoon he went to town, and the man seemed to look forward to his visits. Perhaps they were a change from the usual woman customer, or maybe Mr. Ali enjoyed his role as teacher. He spoke English and Spanish well and helped us a lot.

We got to the corner and waited for the bus. One almost always came along within two or three minutes, and some-times two could be seen coming down the long street at the same time. Then they would race each other trying to get to the corner first. There were at least three bus lines on the same route, and they were in bitter competition.

This afternoon, in the pouring rain, one turned the corner several blocks up the street just as another skidded around it, and they drove neck and neck on the wet pavement. We held our breath as we watched.

Both busses slithered to a stop in front of us. We chose the nearest one to get in out of the rain as fast as possible and didn't realize until were were on it that it had wooden seats and a frustrated racer for a driver.

We held on for life as he careened down the broad thoroughfare, evidently jubilant over snatching two riders from the other bus. He wove in and around cars and trucks, and we peered ahead hoping to see someone waiting on a corner so he would have to stop.

We were out of luck. It was still early, and the after-dinner rush hadn't begun. Everything downtown closed at noon and didn't open again until two-thirty or three o'clock. In some cases they remained closed until four, so most people didn't go shopping until that hour.

Mr. Ali often opened the bazaar early. When we staggered off the bus and down the two blocks to his shop, we were glad to see him standing in the doorway, his favorite spot.

"Mr. Stevens! You did come. And your wife too." He beamed when he saw us, then chided me for staying away so long.

"My husband won't let me come," I teased. "He knows I can't walk in this place without buying something."

It was almost the truth. The first time we went in we bought several things to send home as well as some trinkets for ourselves. We didn't bargain with him but paid the price he asked. After giving him the money Howard stood talking for a while. They discovered they both were masons. As we started to leave, Mr. Ali called the children back. He opened the glass display case in the middle of the floor with a key from his key chain and took out an exquisite little water buffalo carved from ivory. He handed it to Cathy saying, "It's very old and valuable, so take good care of it."

We protested, but he raised his hand and said, "I want to do it. I charged you too much for those things. It won't happen again."

As far as we know, he gave us very fair prices on everything else we bought from him. If he did take unfair advantage of us, it was done in a very charming way.

This afternoon he could hardly contain his excitement. He had received a chest he wanted to show us. It was so intricately carved that from a distance it appeared textured. But close examination showed the details of countless figures, men and animals, each panel telling a story.

Like a child he showed us how the chest opened showing

another chest and inside it another, and so on. At each stage
he had to unlock the next piece, and even the lock was hidden
or disguised by the carving. After several such manuevers the
last opening revealed an interior about the size of a small shoe
box. The wood was satiny to the touch and was probably teak,
although it was as dark as mahogany.

I was fascinated. "It is so beautiful. Was it made for a
special purpose?"

Mr. Ali said, "I don't know unless it is a jewelry box. It came
with some things I ordered. And when I saw it at customs, I
thought you'd be interested in it."

Howard replied, "Of course we are. But we could never
afford anything like that."

The swarthy man smiled. "It isn't for sale. I'll keep it here
for display. But I thought you'd enjoy seeing it. You like
beautiful things so much."

He was right. And with his help we had been able to
acquire a few beautiful things on a limited budget. He had
directed us to several places where we found water color
paintings of the country for just a few cents and to another
shop where we bought a wood carving. We felt that we had a
friend in the dark-skinned Indian from across the world, and
we were grateful for him.

We had some interesting theological discussions. Mr. Ali
never admitted strict adherence to any religion, although he
enjoyed the conversations. One day he introduced Howard
to a friend of his, a Costa Rican whom he felt needed help.

After the introduction he said, "Tell him what you believe. I
think he needs it."

His was a quizzical approach to life, and his perch in the
front door of his shop helped him in the endless observations
of the perplexities of the human race. We left him that

afternoon polishing his chest and contemplating the possibility of beauty being the supreme goal in life.

After a little more window shopping, we got home in time for supper, got the children ready for bed, and started studying again. I thought about the day: Had we wasted it? I wondered. Somehow I felt satisfied with it although we had achieved little that was obvious. But we had walked with one of God's children, one far removed from the usual way of life. I bowed my head and thanked God for his goodness in giving us such relationships with others. And I prayed for Mr. Ali, that his love of beauty might become love for the One who gave us beautiful things.

Chapter 14

Before we left the United States, we were the object of a lot of interest—some sympathetic and some just curious. There seemed to be certain questions we could expect. One of the most common was, "You aren't really going to take those two precious little girls with you, are you?"

I answered that one sincerely and earnestly at first. After a while I would say, trying to smile, "Oh, it's pretty civilized from what we're told."

Other questions frequently encountered were something like these: "I just don't understand it. Why are you going as missionaries to a Christian nation? Don't those people believe in God? Don't they believe in Jesus too?" Usually, before I could form an answer, the skepticism continued: "Why I've got Catholic friends, and I know they're Christians."

When I was able to break in, I tried to assure my questioner that I had Catholic friends also, and many of them were better Christians than I would ever be. But I had to continue with the explanation that the Catholics of our acquaintance were far different from those living in other countries. In many cases there is so much superstition superimposed upon their religion that it bears little resemblance to Christianity.

All this I believed, but sometimes I, myself, wondered how

we could fail to accuse ourselves of proselytizing. I had been in Costa Rica only a few months before I realized that what we were doing could not be considered in that light at all. We could hardly help trying to change someone when he had no faith to start with.

The parades during Holy Week brought us a new awareness of the little faith those around us had. There were parades all week. Much planning and work went into each of them, and the people turned out in great crowds to watch and follow. Each day there was depicted some event leading up to Jesus' crucifixion. Live models were used to represent Roman soldiers, the apostles, and angels. These angels were young girls dressed in swirling garments of pink, blue, and white. They were carried on small platforms, borne on the shoulders of four men and surrounded by mounds of tulle that gave the spectator the impression that the girls floated on clouds.

A statue of Christ was used. As the week progressed, a crown of thorns was added and the form was bent under the weight of the cross. It was impossible to look at the tortured body and deeply lined face without drawing back in horror. Blood streamed in great rivulets from his head, and dark eyes peered from deep sockets.

One parade was in honor of Veronica, she who was supposed to have met Christ on the way with his cross and, feeling sympathy for him, wiped his face. The cloth she used is said to have come away bearing the miraculous imprint of his face in three views. The people have great love for Veronica, and it is an honor to be the young girl chosen to represent her. The purported good deed was acted out in detail, and it was one of the highlights of the week.

Each of the parades followed a pattern. First came the band. Then the altar boys walked in front of the priests, one of them waving burning incense and another beating a clanging, dissonant noise on a tin drum. These odd exercises were meant to drive away the evil spirits as the paraders marched down the streets.

Behind the priests came the soldiers who formed a guard, lining the streets and keeping the onlookers separated from the parade as it passed. Men dressed as the different apostles walked in front of the platform carrying Jesus. Mary, usually a statue too, occupied a place of honor and was carried by nuns on a wooden platform. The little angels followed her, then the people fell into place behind, walking with bowed heads, those of the women covered with shawls.

On Good Friday there were two parades. One showed Christ nailed to the cross. In late afternoon the second one began, and I stood there with tears sliding down my cheeks as I watched man's image of our Lord. He was dead, enclosed in a glass coffin, his hands folded on his breast. The atmosphere was somber, and the people walked along in sadness. Christ was dead.

That was the last parade. We waited in vain for one on Easter morning. We were told that Christ's body was removed from the coffin and placed again on the cross that hung in the church, his usual position all through the year. It would stay there until the following Holy Week, when it would be taken down only to be crucified again. No resurrection was depicted.

As I stood watching one of the demonstrations so pagan in its interpretation, I noticed several small boys near me become very interested in my conversation with the children. I was attempting to explain to them some of the things we were seeing and the boys, on hearing a strange tongue, came closer.

Finally one of them said, "You're a devil, aren't you?"

I looked down at him thinking surely I had misunderstood. A witch, maybe, I thought. I smoothed my hair and tried to smile pleasantly as I asked, "A what?"

Cathy, being helpful, said, "He thinks you're a devil, Mama." Karen giggled and Cathy joined her. I shushed them and asked the boy, "Why do you think I'm a devil?" Curiously, I waited for his answer.

All the little boys snickered, and one or two of them pushed at the one who had spoken first. Evidently he was to be their spokesman.

He shuffled back and forth, then said, "The priest said you were."

I must have looked amazed. I didn't know the priest knew me.

The child went on. "He said you were a devil because you don't believe in Mary."

I said, "Of course I believe in Mary. The Bible tells us all about her, you know."

He didn't know but he continued bravely, "And you don't believe in saints and you're going to hell. Devils live in hell." He gulped when he said the last part, but he got it out.

I hesitated. I wanted so badly to say the right thing. I looked down the block and saw one of the evangelists who was in Costa Rica for the simultaneous crusades sitting on the steps in front of our house. He was the guest of our next-door neighbors and was watching the parade from that spot. He was from Texas and completely bilingual.

I said, "Boys, are you afraid of me?"

They shook their heads. "Would you be afraid to walk down the street with a devil to that blue house?" They looked at each other, but no one wanted to be a coward. So we took off down the street, a large she-type devil trailed by a crowd of scared little boys.

When we got within hailing distance of the preacher, I called him over and told him what had happened. He sat down on the curb with them, and they talked for over an hour.

Nothing was changed for them in that moment, but he had sown a seed. When they started off, every one of the boys turned to wave.

Chapter 15

Having been to the Pacific side of Costa Rica on our trip to Puntarenas, we had a desire to visit the Caribbean. A short holiday several weeks before we were to leave the country gave us an opportunity to visit Limon. We had a choice of going by air or by train. Flying from San José to the port city of Limon was only a matter of thirty minutes, and the trip by train would take several hours. We had no problem at all deciding in favor of the train as it would take us through some of the wildest portions of Costa Rica.

The train had two fares, first and second class. The ticket seller gave us no choice. He said, "You'll want first class."

Howard said, "Now wait a minute. Why do you think we want first class? Maybe we prefer to go second."

The man shook his head. "No, señor. First class." He stamped the tickets and handed them to Howard, telling him the price.

I had to tug at my enraged husband's arm to get him to pay the man and leave without making a scene. "You didn't want to go second class, did you?" I asked.

"No, I didn't. But I wanted the option of saying which I prefer." He stuck out his lip, parodying a spoiled child, and we both laughed.

When the train pulled into the station, we saw what the ticket seller meant. There was one first class coach. As far as we could determine, the cars were identical and the seats the same as those in the second class coaches. But there was one difference. We were alone in our car. All the people standing around had made a rush for seats in the other cars and were packed in as tightly as possible—three or four people wedged into seats meant for two, standing in the aisles, and sitting on boxes and suitcases. Pigs were tied by rope to the back of the seats, and chickens tucked under arms or sticking their heads out of flimsy wooden crates took up the little space left. Children were already squalling, and vendors were making a good profit selling candy, fruit, and soft drinks. We almost felt lonesome looking in on the sociability engendered by the close proximity of it all.

Cathy and Karen were in full possession of our car by the time the train pulled out of the station. It was the last coach and had a small observation platform. When we made the first stop in Cartago, another family got on to share our first class transportation with us. They, too, were on their way to the coast, and their children and ours played back and forth for most of the trip.

Howard and I sat on the edge of our seats watching the changing scenery. We used the benches on the observation deck much of the time, especially when we began to make the descent through the mountains. I had made him promise not to get off at any unscheduled stops, so he hung precariously from the railing several times to get the camera view he wanted. His camera was in danger of falling once or twice as he swung back onto the seat, but I didn't change my mind. The camera was more expendable than he.

The train wound slowly through rain forests on tracks high

above the tumultuous rivers that widened as other rivers joined them to make one wide band of writhing, tossing water. There was vegetation, without a break, as far as the eye could see. The only sign of man, apart from the railroad tracks, was in the narrow strip along the sides of the railroad itself. Occasionally we passed small communities built as close to the tracks as possible with the jungle pressing in at their backs.

Many of the houses were built up on high stilts and covered with thatched roofs. Banana trees and coconut palms grew in profusion near the houses. When we began seeing small buildings with roofs only three or four feet from the ground, my first thought was—pygmies? Then noticing tracks like railway spurs leading into the structures, we became curious enough to ask the man and woman in the coach with us, "Excuse us, but can you tell us what those buildings are?"

They laughed and put down their magazines. The scenery seemed to be of only casual interest to them as they had scarcely looked up from the time we left Cartago.

The man said, "Those are cacao sheds. The beans are placed on racks in the sun to dry, and the racks can be run under the shelter in a hurry if it starts to rain."

We thanked him for the information and Howard started taking some pictures. Cacao beans! I called Cathy and Karen and said, "Look, girls, at those beans drying out there. That's what we get chocolate from."

Karen said, "I'm hungry, Mommy."

Cathy said, "I want a Milky Way. I haven't had a Milky Way since we left Georgia."

I sighed. "Forget it." They skipped off to play in the back corner bench again, and I thought, We might as well stop deluding ourselves that we make all these excursions so they can see things and be educated.

Mr. Muñoz, the man who had answered our question, followed Howard out to the observation platform where he was taking pictures. Now they were sitting there talking. His wife turned to me and said, "You're Americans, aren't you?"

I nodded yes and she said, "I thought so." I immediately thought: Uh-huh, that poor Spanish again and with this accent, how could she miss?

But she added, "I thought so because you only have two children."

I looked at her brood. There were three girls and four boys, one a small baby that the maid had taken care of so far. Mrs. Muñoz looked to be in her late twenties.

She laughed. "You Americans! Don't you like children?

The return of the men saved me from an answer. They began telling us about seeing a boy shinny up one of the tall coconut trees, and the question didn't come up again.

A vendor came through the car, and I thought someone had fallen off the train when Karen first yelled. I jumped to my feet as she came tearing down the aisle hollering, "Look, look, look!" She had a box of Cracker Jacks in her hand, the first we had seen since we left the States.

We bought each girl a box and asked the boy where he had gotten them. He said he was able to buy them in Limon when boats came through carrying things like that. The cost was almost twice the usual amount, but in view of the long boat trip, we didn't complain. For weeks afterwards when our trip to Limon was mentioned, the children's eyes would light up. "Yeah, that's where we got the Cracker Jacks!" Ah, culture and the broadening experience of travel!

The train got to Limon on time, more or less—being only an hour late. Even the conductor looked pleased and commented on his train several times while helping us disembark. We found a taxi and asked to be taken to the hotel that had been recommended to us. The taxi driver looked at us a little oddly, but we were so used to being looked at oddly and misunderstood everytime we opened our mouths that we didn't think too much about it. It took the man a few minutes to get our bags stashed away in the trunk and us fitted into his small cab. He drove up the street, turned the corner, then another, and pulled up in front of the hotel. We were probably 200 yards from the train station.

The hotel was on the ocean as we had been told, but a narrow street and a sea wall separated it from the water. There was no beach, only a jagged line of rocks. The waves were breaking over the rocks sending up a tall spray, and we could hardly get the children inside. The sky and the water were the same shade of gray in the late afternoon light. It reminded me of some early water colors I had done, using washes of grays and whites, with the only accents in black.

The hotel was old, but our room was large and comfortable. It overlooked the sea, and the noise of the sea gulls making wide sweeps and dips above the surf came in loudly through the open windows. By the time we unpacked we were all ready for dinner, so we cleaned up rapidly and went down to the dining room.

All the way down the stairs Cathy and Karen kept informing us what they wanted to eat. The long trip and the salt air had given them enormous appetites, and we would have had a twelve course dinner if they could have had all they thought they wanted. We entered a large dining room with tables placed along the windows that overlooked the sea wall.

A waitress seated us and handed each person a large white napkin that matched the immaculate table cloth. She left and came back shortly with bowls and a giant tureen of soup.

Howard looked perplexed and said, "May we see the menu?"

She said, "But there is no menu. You want to eat supper, don't you?" We all said yes in a very positive way, and she left again to bring us large slabs of bread and butter to go with the soup.

We bowed our heads, thanking God for our safe journey and for the food. Cathy was praying. When she said "Amen," Karen added, "And thank you for the Cracker Jacks, too."

The soup was hot and so delicious I had to call a halt after seconds for everyone. "I think there will be something else."

The girl came from the kitchen carrying a large tray. Our plates were heaped high with food, and additional bowls of food were placed on the table. We had fish fillets almost two inches thick. They had been broiled to a crisp, buttery turn. Along with the fish was a salad of tomatoes and cucumbers, fluffy white rice, and carrots cooked with fresh green peas.

Our long, tall glasses of iced tea were constantly refilled. We didn't indulge in dinner time conversation that night. Even the little one almost licked the platter clean. The waitress asked, "Are you sure you've had enough?" before removing the bowls and platters. We almost groaned when she came back with dessert, a type of floating pudding.

For a while we sat in utter contentment. Then a man and woman came in, looked around, and sat down at one of the tables near the entrance. I did not hear any of the conversation between them and the waitress, but in a moment she came over and said, "Forgive me for asking, but they do not speak Spanish, and I don't know what they want. Could you help me?" She asked me and, while Howard would have made a better translator, I followed her to the table.

I introduced myself and said, "I'll be glad to help if I can."

The man said, "All we want is two orders of shrimp. I don't see why she can't understand that!" he added irritably.

I told the waitress what they wanted and she said, "But we aren't serving shrimp tonight. We may have it tomorrow night."

When I passed this information on, I added that the dinner they were serving was excellent. The man got up, flung his napkin down and said, "They told us on the ship that shrimp was a speciality in this port."

I turned to the waitress again, "Is there any place in town where they might be able to find shrimp?"

She thought for a moment and suggested one place. When I told them, he cursed rudely and grabbed his companion by the arm. They hurried out of the dining room.

The girl blinked back her tears. "Did I do something wrong, Señora?" I patted her arm and looked at the departing backs of my fellow North Americans. "No, you did nothing wrong. They're just in a hurry."

We had been looking forward to returning to the States, and as the time was close at hand we had been making some exciting plans. Suddenly I wondered, Have I forgotten so fast? Is everyone like that?

I went back to our table. Finally we thanked our waitress for a delightful meal, complimented her on her good service, and left for a walk around town.

At the first light the next morning Cathy and Karen awoke wanting to go swimming. The air was so brisk I huddled back under the blankets and begged them to read or play awhile. I had almost dozed off when they began to plead the second time. So Howard and I reluctantly got up and dressed. We did persuade them to wait until after breakfast, hoping it would be warmer by then.

The man at the desk gave us directions to a small beach not too far from the hotel. We walked around the sea wall until we came to steps leading down to a beach no larger than our back yard. The sand was clean and white, and there were rocks of a comfortable size to sit on lining the edges. The children swam in the clear water and played in the sand while Howard and I looked for shells. We had been there about thirty minutes when we were joined by a gang of children, none older than seven or eight. They hit the beach, shucked out of their clothes as unconcernedly as if they had been at home in the privacy of their bathrooms, and plunged into the water. The small, brown bodies were entrancing, and the girls seemed more interested in their water battles than their suitless state. One little girl seemed to be a self-appointed arbitrator between the boys. If they started fighting with too much sincerity, she would grab them by their ears and push them under the water.

I was interested in seeing what they would do about putting their clothes back on when they were ready to go, since they had no towels. It was no problem at all. They came out of the water, lined up, and raced back and forth on the beach until they were dry. Then they put on their clothes and raced off along the sea wall.

After our morning swim we spent the rest of the day looking around the small seaport. On one corner we were stopped by a man selling coconut milk. He chopped off a slice from the top of the coconut with his machete, stuck in a couple of straws, and handed it to Karen. Then we all had to have our own coconuts full of delicious milk.

We left the next day. The trip home by train took longer because, according to the conductor, we were going uphill. It makes sense, I guess.

Chapter 16

Our days had an easy fluidity of design. My eyes popped open each morning at six o'clock to a world shimmering in beauty. We had a view of the mountains from our bedroom windows, and in the clarity of the early morning light we had a feeling of being able to reach out and rub the violet blue and turquoise of each rippling back. There was no sleeping in the light that came up across the tall ranges each sunrise, so alive and instant. One moment it would be softly dark; the next, the whole world was bathed and refreshed in the pulsating newness.

After classes in the morning and lunch, I went to the bedroom to rest and study. Howard went to town. One of his favorite excursions was to the barber shop. There he had ample opportunity to talk and was always meeting someone besides the barbers with whom he could converse. One day he came home quite elated. He had met a young man from Peru who was trying to get to the United States. At that time our field of service was to be Peru, so we were both glad to find someone from that country who might answer our many questions.

Howard invited him for dinner at six-thirty one evening. At seven he still hadn't arrived, and we doubted that Howard had been clear enough in his directions. Then about seven-fifteen we saw him moseying down the street; and although I had not met Fernando, I knew at first glance it must be he.

The young man was tall, extremely thin, with a pure Indian cast to his features. He was dressed neatly in slacks, shirt, and a knitted Peruvian sweater.

He thanked us for asking him to our home, and we thanked him for coming. There was talk of the weather and how he liked Costa Rica, then we sat down to eat. We asked questions and listened to a rapid torrent of words as he told of his home. We couldn't understand parts of what he said, but we caught something of the feeling behind the words.

His desire was to become an aeronautical engineer, return to Peru, and help raise the economic level of his people. He had come as far as Costa Rica on his own money and was waiting to hear from a man in the States who had promised him passage and a sponsorship for his studies there. Fernando wanted help in writing the man a letter as he had heard nothing from him in weeks. The letter was written, and Fernando left to mail it promising to visit us later.

He came again and again. He was interested in our religion because he had never talked with anyone outside his church. On one occasion he said, "I don't really care too much for my church. I go because my family has always gone. What else is there to do?"

"What else is there to do?" The question haunted us. Howard wanted so desperately to share with Fernando the deep joy we had and that others knew. He began searching for all the literature he could find printed in Spanish and pertaining to salvation. He also passed on to Fernando study course books, autobiographies, and, of course, the Bible. Our young friend would come with questions and doubts, with challenges and fears. Howard sat at the dining table with him, night after night, dictionary in one hand and the Bible in the other.

Fernando was so interested. There was no doubting his sincere wish to find a better way than he knew. But a lifetime of teachings blocked him, and a limited ability in Fernando's language blocked Howard.

Week after week passed, and the long-sought letter from the U. S. did not come. We wrote again; still no response. Fernando's funds were running low, and he could not enter the States without sponsorship and help with his schooling. We could only sympathize with him and welcome him into our home when he came.

Late one night he and Howard sat talking again. Fernando said, "Tell me, just one more time." My husband didn't have to ask what the young man wanted to hear. As simply as possible he presented the plan of salvation, pointing out Scripture verses and asking Fernando to read them aloud.

The doubts fell away in one miraculous moment. They fell away because he had continued to read, search, study, ask, and pray. He bowed his head and prayed again, placing himself and his life in God's hands. His dark eyes glittered with tears as he said, "God does care. He does care. I know. I belong to him now."

Bill Gray came over soon after that. Knowing that sharing one's salvation experience helps to crystallize it, Howard asked Fernando to tell Bill what had happened to him. In faltering words, groping for expressions unfamiliar to him, he recounted his long dissatisfaction with his life, the seeking and unrest, and now his joy in finding the Saviour who had forgiven his sins and loved him.

It was an up-and-down time for Fernando in the weeks that

followed. He joined a Baptist church and overflowed with ideas for the work. Some were good, others were so poorly conceived that his enthusiasm was annoying to some people. But he tried, and he studied constantly.

The day we left Costa Rica he was at the airport. The letter had never arrived. He had long since come to realize that it was not coming and that he must make plans to return to Peru.

Meanwhile our plans had changed also. We would not be going to Peru, but to another field of service. Our farewells were based on the knowledge that there was little probability of our seeing each other again. His final words touched our hearts.

"You came to Costa Rica planning to go to Peru. I came to Costa Rica planning to go to the United States. I wanted to become an engineer and go back to my country and help my people. Now, you are not going to Peru. But I am. I will go back in your place, and if God will help me, I will help my people in another way. I will help them by telling them what you have told me. God be with you."

Chapter 17

I think all Americans ought to be required to live outside the United States for awhile. Things that are commonplace become very dear after a few months away from the native land. There is even a tendency to be ashamed of fussing about things like income tax, community drives, and having to serve as den mother. Old-timers tell us that when all the politicians begin to look good and sound plausible, then we'll be past due for a furlough.

We had been out of the States almost eleven months when we were invited, along with all the other North Americans living in Costa Rica, to the annual Fourth-of-July party at the United States ambassador's home. I say "other North Americans" even though I have had it hammered into me that everyone living on the North American continent is a North American and it is an insult to assume that we have priority on that name. There is a word for us in Spanish: *"estadounidense."* But I haven't found a comfortable translation for it yet. "United Statser" sounds like one of Walter Winchell's creations. "United Statsen" looks like a foreign title, and "citizen of the United States" is a bit formidable to use in casual conversation.

We were excited over the idea of a celebration that was to

be one hundred percent American (there I go again—not satisfied with just North America). We had seen fiestas, parades, and festivities of Costa Rica all year. Perhaps we were just a little homesick.

When we arrived at the ambassador's home on the morning of the Fourth, it was misting and cool. I thought, It's going to take a lot to make this seem like a Fourth-of-July celebration in Georgia. But in less than thirty minutes the sun was shining, and we were able to take off our sweaters and raincoats.

There must have been a thousand people milling around the grounds. The home was in one of the lovely suburbs of San José, set back from the road, with a long, circular drive approaching the house. A band was playing marches, and activities were under way in every corner. We stood and listened to the music for awhile, drank Cokes, and ate big bags of popcorn. Then Cathy, who had left us at the gate, came tearing around from the back of the house and said, "Come on! I'm going to be in a race."

Foot races, potato sack races, relay races, and more were going on in full force on the back lawn. The children raced by ages, and Cathy came in second in the group of nine-year-olds. After this victory Howard wandered over to watch a horseshoe match, and Karen and I went into the garage to look at cartoons being shown to children and adults alike. After a year without Bugs Bunny and Donald Duck, Karen would have stayed glued to her chair all day if anyone had just had the patience to show the same cartoons over and over for her. She did turn her head long enough to ask me to please get her one of the ice creams like other children kept wandering in with.

I walked out into the sunlight, blinking from the darkness of the movie room. There were booths for ice cream, peanuts, and popcorn. One was doing a booming business with caramelized peanuts, and soft drinks. A long counter had been set up, and they were beginning to give out hot dogs. I fixed Karen a hot dog, got her a drink, and put the two in the hands she held up when I sat down beside her. The ruse worked. She was so absorbed in the fantasy unfolding before her eyes that she didn't realize what she was eating until the last bite. Then she turned to me. "Mommy, I said an ice cream! What did you give me a hot dog for?"

"For to keep you from getting so full you wouldn't want one. Are you ready for your ice cream now?"

She grinned. "Nope. I'm too full!" And she continued to look at the screen.

The lights flickered, and the young man running the projector said, "All for now. I've got to let this thing cool off."

There were groans from the little ones and relieved sighs from the parents. We got most of the children out without crying by convincing them we could find some other diversion. There was an animated softball game going on, and we located Howard and Cathy cheering for opposite sides. We watched for awhile, then sat down on the ground to eat our hot dogs.

We had just finished when we heard the announcement. "It's time for the pie eating contest. Come one! Come all!"

The girls ran ahead of us. Howard commented, "You know, this will be the first time I've ever seen one in real life."

I said, "Me too. I wish they'd had them when I was a kid."

There weren't too many contestants, but every participant had a dozen people yelling for him. After the first pie there was no question who the winner was going to be. One chubby-faced boy ate as methodically and quietly as a steam shovel biting into the ground. The others floundered and gasped and groaned. He just got down to work and plowed through six pies before he stopped. When he was awarded the prize he said, "I could have done a lot better if you had told me about it before I ate all them hot dogs."

One of the main attractions of the day was the ox cart decorated with red, white, and blue streamers. Painted ox carts are a symbol of Costa Rica, and their owners take great pride in their bright vehicles. Designs are passed down from artist to son and are highly valued. We enjoyed seeing the dozens of carts come by our house during the coffee bean season, going out empty and coming back laden with the dark red berries.

This cart was so festooned with ribbons and crepe paper it was hard to tell anything about its design as the oxen plodded around the circular drive taking the children for a ride. Karen couldn't make up her mind whether or not she wanted to ride, and Cathy felt a little old for it all. When the cart was on the opposite side of the circle from us, it looked very appealing to Karen; but when it came to climbing in behind the animals she would change her mind. She changed it so many times I finally talked her into helping us find a place to sit on the lawn in front of the house so we could hear the speeches when they started.

There were a few short addresses, then the ambassador spoke. He won the hearts of those Costa Ricans present to play in the band and to give the gun salute, by addressing them also, and in Spanish. Then we sang the national anthem and saluted the flag. A deep silence settled over the crowd, and there were few adults able to sing "The Star Spangled

Banner" without swallowing past a couple of very large lumps in their throats.

Then a shout went up as Uncle Sam strode out of the house. He was perfect from the shiny top hat to the striped pants. He carried small flags for all the children; and as each of them took a flag, he fell into place behind Uncle Sam to march around the drive. The band played "The Stars and Stripes Forever," and the children waved the flags over their heads as they marched. Many of the boys and girls had never set foot on United States soil. Others had been away so long they remembered very little about their land. Yet, pride in their country had been carefully nurtured, and the children following Uncle Sam looked like a scene from the Pied Piper.

As the crowd broke up, it started to drizzle again. No one complained. The rain had held off for several hours from its usual schedule, and the day had been perfect. We stood under umbrellas waiting for the busses to come, and I breathed a silent prayer for our country, for its strength, and for the innate goodness of its people. I could have been called anything at that moment as long as it was tagged, "Made in the U. S. A."

Chapter *18*

We had arrived in August for a year's study in San José. Now it was July, and all of us were in a whirl trying to get things in order to leave. Howard walked around talking to himself as he attempted to keep in mind all the things that had to be done. "Exit permits, travel papers, freight allowances, passports, health cards. . . ."

I left all that to him and started to pack. We had brought our things in several foot lockers and despite the fact that the children had outgrown most of their clothes and others had worn out, it didn't seem possible to get all we had back into the same lockers. I packed several, only to find a few hours later that something extremely vital was at the bottom of each one.

I repacked, trying to put in those things which I knew we wouldn't be needing. In one trunk I was fully confident that I had made a wise choice as I packed the box of Christmas decorations we had bought. Then I put some of the souvenirs we were taking home to family and friends on top of that. I finished packing the trunk with clothes Cathy had outgrown and that I was going to save for Karen.

I closed the trunk, locked it, and felt very satisfied until I looked around to see seven more lined up, their emptiness taunting me. But one out of eight wasn't bad, and I began to cheer up. This good feeling lasted until I walked downstairs and found Howard busily wrapping a table in burlap for shipping.

"Honey, I need that ball of heavy twine. Will you get it for me, please?"

I asked, as hope drained away, "You wouldn't know where it is, by any chance?"

"I'm pretty sure it's in the box of Christmas things. We used it to brace the tree, remember?"

I croaked, "I tohught so," and crept back upstairs to undo several hours of work.

It may have been this sense of futility that prompted me to pack three trunks with anything at hand, without contemplating their immediate use. I packed to be packed, to be finished, to be done with it. When I went to bed that night I was exhausted, but I had some hope of our getting the trunks to the airline by the date we had set.

The next morning I crawled out of bed determined to get the other five packed. When I walked into the hall, I stopped in horror. There were the eight trunks lined up as before, each of them completely empty. I gawked at stacks of clothing, piles of toys, columns of books, shoes, things draped from chairs, and spilling off the table, and leaning against the walls. But the trunks were empty.

I shook Howard. He was sleeping peacefully, but that didn't stop me from asking, "What did you do to my trunks? They're empty."

He mumbled something about their not being packed right and went back to sleep. It is my luck to be married to a former navy man. He can pack four cubic yards of anything into two cubic yards without half trying. When he's really determined he can pack it into one. And he was determined this time because he knew how much stuff we had. However, while he is methodical, he is also so slow I knew we would never finish. We'd still be sitting there staring at foot lockers when the new batch of students arrived.

We worked all weekend. I fetched and ran. He packed, repacked, and packed again. The day before we were to leave, he got all eight of them to the airport. They arrived in Georgia several weeks after we did when we were about to despair over living out of the suitcases we had carried with us. But they arrived with everything shipshape.

While we had been in the throes of packing, Howard was also in the turmoil of trying to find a different route back to the States instead of the long trip we had made in coming. He haunted the travel agent's office. There was a flight to Miami that took five hours, but it was scheduled only on certain days that did not fit our plans.

Our agent was a small, neat man with a perpetual smile. He came bouncing up to us one day at school saying, "Amigos, do not carry your worries with you any longer." He spoke English with very little accent and had a charming way of stringing words together.

"I have for you a most ingenious solution to your problem. You go to Panama and from Panama to Miami. Great, huh?"

Howard and I looked at each other. Panama was in the opposite direction from home if we were remembering our geography correctly. But Señor Travel Agent was falling all over himself to tell us the schedule, and in a moment we were smiling too.

The trip to Panama was a little over an hour. From there we could get a jet to Miami and be there in an hour and a half. Planes to Atlanta from Miami left every few hours. The fare would be about the same, and I was enchanted with the idea of not staying on a plane all day.

We were eager to leave. The day arrived, and we were at the airport early. We had gained so much more than a study of Spanish during out year in Costa Rica. The courses we took were wrapped in the philosophy of the people themselves. We learned new ways, many better than we had known. We fell in love with the nationals. We butted heads with our fellow missionaries and learned to love and respect them. We were leaving, not as seasoned missionaries, but with a generous sprinkling of tenderizer.

Even though we were ready to be on our way, nostalgia threatened to overwhelm me when I looked at the dozens of friends from our church in Heredia who had come to tell us good-bye. There was the old desire to leave but also to stay behind—the eternal conflict of the need to move on and the reluctance to break the ties that bind. Then the plane arrived, on time, and we got a strong *abrazo* from everyone and headed south.

San José has a year-round climate of springtime. We were seldom too warm and rarely cold. After a year of experiencing no extremes except in our climbs to the volcanoes, the hot August air of the airport in Panama nearly bowled us over. We gasped for breath and headed quickly for immigrations and customs inside. Overhead fans were turning, but they seemed to make little difference in the heat. We stood in line and were just having our bags checked when we heard an anguished cry from Karen.

She had her hand on the back of her neck under her hair. I looked hurriedly, thinking something had bitten her. But she brought out her hand again, pointed to the perspiration dripping from it, and started crying.

At first we couldn't understand what she was saying, but finally the words came out in an agonized howl, "I'm bleeding white blood, Mommy!"

We spent a day in Panama trying to pack months of sight-seeing into a few hours. The next day we returned to the airport to get on the jet for Miami. When departure time came, we lined up with the other passengers and stood there for over an hour before we were informed over the loud-speaker that the plane would be late in departing. We visited the gift shop and prowled around the small terminal. The flight was called again. Again we lined up and waited.

This time the voice over the loudspeaker apologized, but takeoff would be delayed again. There was no place to eat, so we got some Cokes out of a machine, and I read to the children awhile. One of the passengers walking around outside spotted the jet near the hangar with about half of its seats removed. When he came back and shared this bit of sleuthing with some of us, another man said, "Well, it's possible it's not our plane, you know."

The amateur detective said, "Oh yes it is. They've already got the number posted by the door, and it's ours all right." Several of the men got up and went over to the reservations counter to complain.

I looked at the clock. We had been there since eleven o'clock and it was now a little past three. The children were hungry, so we got some peanuts out of a machine and another drink. The men came back to report, "He knows nothing about it. Or at least that's what he claims." Everyone settled down to wait.

Howard took the girls outside for a walk, and while they were gone, the speaker announced the arrival of a flight from Buenos Aires. People filed into the terminal in silence. They all looked tired. I felt particularly sorry for those dressed in woolens as they came into the heat of the waiting room. Many had left the cold of late winter in South America, and they rapidly drooped in the late afternoon heat. In just a few minutes the public address system crackled again saying, "The flight to Miami is announced. Check your tickets and get in line please."

I dashed out to look for Howard and the girls, and we fell into place. As we boarded the plane the man behind us said, "I've just found out why we've been waiting all this time. They got the plane overhauled, then decided they might as well wait for this bunch coming in from South America that had reservations on to Miami." Our hours of waiting seemed justified by this accommodation to other travelers.

It was almost dark when we flew out of Panama. When we landed in Miami it was late, and the girls were so tired Howard asked the customs official to excuse us. He stayed with the luggage, and we went up by elevator to the hotel within the enormous terminal.

I walked up to the desk and asked for a room for two adults and two children. The clerk asked, "What did you say?"

I repeated my request. He still looked blank. I thought, "Oh, no! I can't communicate!" I suppose my anguish showed because he said, "I understand everything you're saying except one word. You want a room for two 'whats' and two children?"

I burst out laughing. "For myself, my husband, and these two girls."

He said, "Oh. Well, you know we get some odd requests around here, and I didn't know what you might be bringing in."

As he handed me the key I said, "All I'm bringing in besides the luggage that will be coming up shortly is my husband. Okay?"

He grinned and said, "I hope you'll be comfortable."

We got to the room, and I flopped on the bed while Cathy and Karen ran to the television set. I had to browbeat them into bed with the promise that I would wake them in time for the cartoons the next morning.

Our plane left for Atlanta at eight-thirty, so we got up early and let them watch the programs for awhile. If I had anything to say to them I had to come between them and the set, deliberately cutting off their view before the lines of communication between us would clear. It was a hard task to pull them away to catch the plane, but the thought of seeing their grandparents helped.

We were glad to board the plane for the last leg of our journey—the closing of a circle that represented a year of life, of hard work, of joy, and of a continued sense of God's leadership. We had changed. All the changes weren't visible ones for we could see this circle closing, and new, larger ones beginning, moving ever outward. The unknown beckoned, and I was happy knowing that we were following God's divine will for us. Howard caught my eye, and I suppose he was thinking along the same lines because he said, "I know it can't be any better, then I find myself anticipating the next turn in the road." I smiled. We were ready.

For ye shall go out with joy, and be led forth with peace: the mountains and the hills shall break forth before you into singing, and all the trees of the field shall clap their hands (Isa. 55:12).